D1411331

Grill Skills

Professional
Tips for the
Perfect Barbeque

Liselotte Forslin

Mia Gahne

Jan Gradvall

Bengt-Göran Kronstam

Catharina Lindeberg-Bernhardsson

Tove Nilsson

Mia Öhrn

4880 Lower Valley Road • Atglen, PA 19310

THE AUTHORS WOULD LIKE TO THANK

Weber Stephen Nordic, Mateus Stock AB, Hackman, Länna Möbler, Stationen in Uppsala, The English Bookshop, Crêperie Lemoni in Uppsala, Miriam Parkman, Sonja & Rolf Ekman, Ylva Porsklev, Klara Nordlund, Maura at Borgo Muratori in Ligurien, Italy, and also Thea, Klara, and Alex.

OTHER SCHIFFER BOOKS ON RELATED SUBJECTS

The Big
Smoker Book

by Karsten
"Ted" Aschenbrandt
ISBN 978-0-7643-4328-5

Grilling
Like a Champion

by Rudolf Jaeger
ISBN 978-0-7643-4498-5

Great Grilling
& Hot Sauces

by Ralf Nowak
ISBN 978-0-7643-4851-8

© 2015 by Schiffer Publishing, Ltd.

Library of Congress Control Number: 2014956649

Originally published as *Fixa Grillen: Proffsens Bästa Tips för en Lyckad Grillning* by ICA Bokförlag, Stockholm. © 2012 by the authors and ICA Book Publishing, Forma Books Ltd. Translated from the Swedish by Omicron Language Solutions, LLC.

Type set in Traveling Typewriter & Chase

ISBN: 978-0-7643-4768-9
Printed in China

Published by Schiffer Publishing, Ltd.
4880 Lower Valley Road
Atglen, PA 19310
Phone: (610) 593-1777; Fax: (610) 593-2002
E-mail: Info@schifferbooks.com

For our complete selection of fine books on this and related subjects, please visit our website at www.schifferbooks.com. You may also write for a free catalog.

This book may be purchased from the publisher. Please try your bookstore first.

We are always looking for people to write books on new and related subjects. If you have an idea for a book, please contact us at proposals@schifferbooks.com.

Schiffer Publishing's titles are available at special discounts for bulk purchases for sales promotions or premiums. Special editions, including personalized covers, corporate imprints, and excerpts can be created in large quantities for special needs. For more information, contact the publisher.

Original Idea and Project Management: Ingela Holm
Foreword, 30 Commandments for a Grill Master, and Music Tips: Jan Gradvall
Recipes for Classic Bistro Grill, Family Grill Fest, Mediterranean Grill: Liselotte Forslin
Recipes for Barbeque Swedish Style: Mia Gahne
Recipes for Grill for Dinner: Tove Nilsson
Recipes for Grilled Desserts: Mia Öhrn
Table Settings: Catharina Lindeberg-Bernhardsson
Wines: Bengt-Göran Kronstam
Photography: Ulrika Ekblom
Design: Jonas Larsson
Editor: Lena Fieber

CONTENTS

THE GRILL IS ON!

Barbequing isn't only about cooking. Somebody frying a steak in the kitchen doesn't draw a crowd to stand around sipping wine while discussing the issues of the day.

Barbequing is a ritual. The word itself can be traced all the way back to a Caribbean expression that can roughly be translated as "sacred fire."

The fire becomes something bigger, the glow somehow more important.

The barbeque becomes a way to rise above the day-to-day.

A way to connect with what's important in life; like food, friends, and conversation.

And, of course, music and something good to drink.

The more mealtimes that we raise up to become rituals during the year, the easier it becomes to nip negative thoughts in the bud.

The more often you barbeque, the stronger your immune system becomes to all things gray.

Welcome to the party! The grill is on.

Jan Gradvall

30 COMMANDMENTS FOR A GRILL MASTER

Preparations for Grilling

1. Allow the charcoal to absorb the lighter fluid for at least a couple of minutes before lighting. Set light to several places at once. More environmentally friendly alternatives to lighter fluid are lighter cubes or lighter paper.

2. Light the grill half an hour before you start grilling. The charcoal should have time to form a light gray surface of ash.

3. Clean the cooking grill thoroughly using a wire brush before every use. You should ideally do this while the grill's lit, as the heat will burn off the residue.

4. Rub the cooking grill with a little oil — but not so much that it drips onto the coals. Before you place any meat on the grill it should be sufficiently hot, otherwise the meat can stick.

5. Use good quality lump charcoal or briquettes and store them in a dry environment since charcoal easily absorbs moisture. Rake out all the old ashes before adding new charcoal.

6. Lump charcoal or briquettes? Briquettes burn longer and are preferable when grilling large pieces of meat or thick steaks. Briquettes that haven't burnt out can be reused.

7. The connoisseur may choose to use various types of wood, such as hickory and mesquite or pear and apple, to flavor the food.

8. You can even sprinkle herbs over the coals to give the food extra flavor and aroma. Try using rosemary, fennel, bay leaf, or tarragon.

Choice of Grill

9. Make sure that the grill is stable and shielded from the wind The cooking grill should be chromed and height adjustable as well as solid and durable; poor-quality cooking grills tend to have weak bars.

10. A grill with a lid cooks evenly and effectively. Vents allow the hot air to circulate continuously inside the grill and because the heat is evenly distributed there's no need for a rotisserie or height-adjustable cooking grill.

11. If the grill becomes too warm, the temperature can be adjusted using the bottom vents. The top vents should always be open when grilling.

During Grilling

12. Meat and other food should not be used directly from the refrigerator, but should instead be at room temperature when placed on the grill. This allows the food to cook more quickly and evenly.

13. Wipe off excess meat juices or marinade before placing the meat on the grill.

14. Never use a fork when turning the meat: any holes will allow the meat juices to escape. Use tongs instead.

15. Always salt after cooking, never before. Salt, and even spice mixes containing salt, will draw out the juices from the meat.

16. Don't place too much food on the grill at once. This will smother the fire. The heat needs to circulate freely around the food. If you're having a really big party you might need to borrow a neighbor's grill.

17. The distance from the coals affects the cooking time. Thick pieces of meat should be placed higher up than thin ones. Don't try to speed up the cooking time by placing the meat nearer to the coals — this will only result in the meat being undercooked on the inside or burnt and tough.

18. f the fat is still on the meat (for example, on a pork chop), make a small cut at the edge. This will prevent the meat from curling up during cooking.

19. Feel free to use a cooking grill with a finer mesh when cooking smaller items, like shrimp for example. Place it over the existing cooking grill to prevent food from falling through onto the coals.

20. When grilling, don't miss any opportunity to throw some vegetables onto the grill. Grilled vegetables are always tasty. Either put them on skewers, or wrap them in foil and place them in the coals. You can even grill unpeeled onions or corn cobs directly in the coals. Just brush off the ashes after cooking.

21. Grilled halloumi cheese is a real treat and only takes a few minutes.

22. Keep in mind that the various foods on the grill may absorb flavor from each other. Make sure you keep them separated.

23. Food that needs to marinate is best stored in plastic bags. Shake the bag occasionally while the food marinates.

24. Don't throw away extra unused marinade. You can either serve it as a sauce, warmed through and mixed with crème fraiche, or freeze it until the next barbeque. A marinade will keep in the refrigerator for one week, or in the freezer for up to 3 months.

When It's Almost Done

25. Turn the meat when it begins to sweat. When pink meat juices begin to run from the grilled meat then the meat is pink inside. Remove from the grill if you want medium rare, or continue to cook for well done.

26. Prod the meat with tongs (not with a fork) when it's almost done. The resistance when pressing down on the meat reveals how it looks inside. Soft meat will be bloody, while if it bounces back then it will be pink. If it's hard then it will be well done.

27. Fish should not be grilled for too long. Be precise with the cooking time, as the fish can easily dry out. Oily fish such as salmon and mackerel are therefore always the easiest to grill. The fish is ready when you can flake the flesh with a fork or when it easily comes away from the bone.

28. If you've wrapped the fish in aluminum foil, open up the foil with 5 minutes of the cooking time remaining. The fish will then take on the smoky flavor of the grill. Bear in mind that fish and other items wrapped in foil require more cooking time.

29. Stick a skewer in the vegetables. If it goes through them then they're ready. After grilling, leave the vegetables in their foil wrapping on top of the grill to keep them warm.

30. Whatever you do, don't stress out! Grilling takes time. The great thing about a barbeque is just taking it easy while you're hanging around the grill.

GRILL FOR DINNER

Juicy cuts of meat, crisp salads, tasty dips, and the reek of smoke. Yes, barbequing has always been close to my heart. As often as possible my summer evenings revolve around the grill. Out sailing, at home in the garden, in the park, or on a terrace downtown, dinner around the barbeque is the most delightful way to spend time with friends in the summer. Come sunshine or summer rain, I always barbeque!

Tove Nilsson

TOVE'S TOP GRILL TIPS

1. Light the grill plenty of time ahead, around 30 minutes in advance. Wait until the coals are a perfect gray color and the embers are red hot.

2. Make sure that the cooking grill is hot enough so that the food doesn't stick to the bars.

3. Don't turn the meat too often! It should have a fine caramelized surface that's full of flavor and keeps the meat juicy. If you turn the meat too often there's a risk that it'll overcook and become dull and tasteless.

4. Soak wooden skewers in water for at least 20 minutes to prevent burning.

5. Feel free to leave the descaled skin on fish, since this will help prevent it from sticking to the grill so easily. The skin will be really crisp and tasty.

6. Skewered fish is best grilled in an oiled grill basket to prevent small pieces from falling into the coals if they come loose from the skewer.

7. You can use either the direct or indirect grilling method. With direct grilling, the most common method, the coals are distributed evenly across the bed of the grill. This method is used for grilling skewers, smaller pieces of meat, fish, and other items that don't require long cooking times. For indirect grilling a ring of charcoal is built up around the edges of the grill, leaving the center empty. This method is used for larger cuts of meat, whole chickens, or anything else that needs a long cooking time under a lid.

Jerk Chicken

4 Servings

Jerk is a spice mix from Jamaica with the sweet, intense taste of allspice, cinnamon, and nutmeg. The chicken becomes almost black when grilled due to the caramelization of the dark muscovado sugar together with all the spices. The chicken is butterflied so it can be grilled more quickly.

Instructions

1. Mix the spices, sugar, ginger, vinegar, oil, and salt.
2. Dry the chicken and cut all the way down one side of the backbone, then flatten it like a "butterfly." Rub in the spice mix over the whole chicken.
3. Grill the chicken using indirect heat with lid on for 30 minutes. Turn a few times during grilling.
4. Check that the chicken is ready by cutting into it. If the meat juices are clear and transparent then it is cooked. Serve with yogurt and a dash of olive oil

2 tsp allspice

$1\frac{1}{2}$ tsp dried thyme

2 tsp ground cinnamon

$\frac{1}{5}$ tsp ground nutmeg

$\frac{1}{2}$ tsp freshly ground black pepper

2 tbsp dark muscovado sugar

$1\frac{1}{2}$ tbsp ginger, grated

3 tsp white wine vinegar

1 tbsp olive oil

$1\frac{1}{2}$ tsp salt

1 whole chicken

Sweet Potato Salad with Mango & Lime

4 Servings

Sweet potato salad goes well with jerk chicken, skewered grilled fish (page 43), or grilled pork tenderloin with Caribbean BBQ sauce (page 18).

Directions

1. Preheat the oven to 400 degrees F (200 degrees C).
2. Peel and cut the sweet potatoes into wedges. Toss with oil. Season with salt and pepper. Roast in the middle of the oven for 30 minutes.
3. Peel and cube the mangoes. Finely slice the green onions and chili pepper.
4. Allow the sweet potatoes to cool then mix with the mango, green onions, chili, and lime juice. Garnish with whole cilantro leaves and salt flakes. Serve with lime wedges if desired.

2 sweet potatoes

1 tbsp olive oil

$\frac{1}{2}$ tsp salt

freshly ground black pepper

2 mangoes

3 green onions

1 chili pepper

1 lime + 1 optional for serving

1 bunch cilantro

salt flakes

MUSIC TIPS

Wingless Angels –
Wingless Angels

Keith Richards from
The Rolling Stones jams
with some old Jamaican
Rastafarian musicians by
the campfire on a sandy
beach in heaven.

Grilled Corn on the Cob
with Spiced Butter

4-6 servings

Spiced butters are great with grilled corn but also go well with meat or grilled fish. The ears of corn should be grilled for 8-10 minutes.

Directions

1. Whisk the butter in a bowl together with all the remaining ingredients until fluffy, preferably with an electric whisk.

2. Serve immediately, or form the butter into a roll in plastic wrap and store in the refrigerator.

Herb butter

$3\frac{1}{2}$ tbsp (50 g) butter at room temperature

2 tbsp finely chopped herbs, e.g., thyme, parsley, rosemary, sage, or tarragon

1 garlic clove, grated

$\frac{1}{2}$ a lemon, zest finely grated

Smoked chili butter with sesame oil

$3\frac{1}{2}$ tbsp (50 g) butter at room temperature

1 tsp smoked paprika

$\frac{1}{2}$ tsp chili flakes

$\frac{1}{2}$ tsp sesame oil

Parmesan and truffle butter

$3\frac{1}{2}$ tbsp (50 g) butter at room temperature

$\frac{1}{4}$ c ($\frac{1}{2}$ dl) finely grated parmesan

$\frac{1}{2}$ tsp truffle oil

Clockwise from top: parmesan and truffle butter, smoked chili butter with sesame oil, herb butter.

Kebab Skewers

Spicy kebabs that are great to serve with red cabbage salad, Greek beet salad on page 19, or feta cheese dip on page 29.

Directions

1. Mix the ground meat, egg, grated garlic, spices, harissa, and salt.
2. Form the meat mixture around the skewers and grill, turning occasionally, for about 10 minutes.

1 lb 2 oz (500 g) ground lamb or beef
1 egg
1 garlic clove, grated
1 tsp ground cumin
1 tsp ground coriander
$\frac{1}{2}$ tsp dried mint
$\frac{1}{2}$-1 tbsp harissa
$1\frac{1}{2}$ tsp salt

Red Cabbage Salad with Mint and Lemon

Crisp red cabbage with a tart lemon dressing, fresh mint, and salty feta cheese.

Directions

1. Shred the cabbage thinly with a grater.
2. Whisk together finely grated lemon zest, lemon juice, honey, oil, and salt.
3. Mix together with the cabbage and allow to stand for at least 15 minutes.
4. Top the salad with whole mint leaves and crumbled feta cheese. Season freely with freshly ground black pepper.

$\frac{1}{2}$ head of red cabbage
1 lemon, juice and zest
1 tbsp honey
1 tbsp olive oil
1 tsp salt flakes
1 bunch green mint
5.5 oz (150 g) feta cheese
freshly ground black pepper

MUSIC TIPS

Fatoumata
Diawara –
Fatou

Soul from Mali.
Like extra fuel
for the fire when
the party looks
like it may start
dying down.

Herby Lamb Kebabs

4 servings

These lamb kebabs will be at their best if the meat is allowed to marinate in the herbs and garlic overnight.

Directions

1. Dice the meat into cubes, about 1 1/4 inches by 1 1/4 inches.

2. Peel and crush the garlic. Mix together garlic, herbs, wine, and oil. Allow the meat to marinate in the mixture for at least 30 minutes but preferably overnight in the refrigerator.

3. Season with salt and pepper, and skewer. Grill for 10-15 minutes turning occasionally.

Ingredients
1 lb 12 oz (800 g) lamb sirloin
3 garlic cloves
2 tbsp fresh rosemary, chopped
2 tbsp fresh thyme, chopped
$\frac{1}{4}$ c ($\frac{1}{2}$ dl) dry white wine
1 tbsp olive oil
freshly ground black pepper

Caribbean BBQ Sauce

8 servings

A rich grill sauce with a taste of ginger, allspice, cloves, and smoked chili. The chipotle chili is a smoked, dried chili pepper that should be available from well-stocked supermarkets. If you can't obtain these then use a regular red chili pepper instead.

Directions

1. Steep the chipotle chili in boiling water for around 10 minutes then finely chop. If you're using a red chili, deseed and finely chop.

2. Fry one tablespoon of chopped chili, together with the onion, ginger and spices, in oil. Add the rest of the ingredients and cook, covered, for around 15 minutes. Remove the lid and allow to cook for a further 10 minutes.

3. Mix to a fine sauce with a hand blender. Store in a clean glass jar or tin. Keep cool; the sauce can be stored for up to 2 weeks in the refrigerator.

Ingredients
1 chipotle chili or $\frac{1}{2}$ red chili pepper
$\frac{1}{2}$ yellow onion, finely chopped
2 tbsp fresh ginger, finely chopped
1 tsp ground allspice
$\frac{1}{5}$ tsp ground nutmeg
2 cloves
2 tsp smoked paprika
1 can (14.5 oz / 400 g) crushed tomatoes
2 tbsp tomato puree
$\frac{1}{2}$ c (1 dl) water
4 tbsp muscovado or brown sugar
3 tbsp red wine vinegar
1 tsp salt

Souvlaki with Greek Beet Salad

4 servings

Wonderfully good pork marinated in lemon and served with a beet, oregano, and feta cheese salad.

Directions

1. Cook the beets in boiling salted water until soft, around 30–40 minutes depending on their size.
2. Cut the meat into approximately ¾-inch cubes, and mix with finely grated lemon zest, grated garlic, and 1 tablespoon olive oil. Season with salt and pepper.
3. Skewer the cubes of meat and grill for 10–15 minutes, turning occasionally.
4. Peel and slice the beets. Layer beets, red onion, feta cheese, and oregano on a plate. Drizzle with 1 tablespoon lemon juice and 2 tablespoons olive oil. Season with salt and pepper.
5. Serve the kebabs with the beet salad and a dollop of yogurt.

Ingredients
1 lb 12 oz (800 g) beets
1 lb 12 oz (800 g) pork fillets
1 lemon, zest and juice
1 garlic clove, grated
1 tbsp + 2 tbsp olive oil
salt
freshly ground black pepper
1 red onion, sliced
5.5 oz (150 g) feta cheese, diced
1 tsp dried oregano
$\frac{3}{4}$ c ($1\frac{1}{2}$ dl) Greek yogurt

Grilled Ratatouille Salad with Halloumi

4 servings

Halloumi, crisp and tasty, is perfect for the grill.

Directions

1. Slice the eggplant and mix with 1 teaspoon salt in a bowl. Allow to stand for around 10 minutes.
2. Slice the bell peppers and zucchini. Peel the onions and slice into wedges. Halve the tomatoes.
3. Grill the vegetables, on a skewer if preferred, and place on a large plate, skewers removed.
4. Slice and grill the halloumi, then mix the cheese with the salad.
5. Whisk together the grated garlic, oil, vinegar, and mustard. Add the fresh herbs and drizzle the dressing over the salad.
6. Finally, add the spinach. Season with salt flakes and pepper.

Ingredients
1 eggplant
1 tsp salt
2 bell peppers
1 zucchini
2 red onions
6 tomatoes
10.5 oz (300 g) halloumi
1 garlic clove, grated
3 tbsp olive oil
1 tbsp red wine vinegar
1 tsp Dijon mustard
1 tbsp finely chopped herbs, e.g., thyme or rosemary
3 oz (80 g) spinach leaves
salt flakes
freshly ground black pepper

Quesadillas with
Sweet Potato and Cilantro

4-6 servings

A tasty snack around the grill: Mexican tortillas filled with sweet potato, corn, and cheese. Mmmm!

Directions

1. Peel and slice the potato into small pieces. Boil in salted water until soft.

2. Deseed and finely chop the chili pepper.

3. Mash the sweet potato and mix in the chili, cheese, corn, and chopped cilantro. Season with half a teaspoon of salt.

4. Spread the mixture over half of a large tortilla. Fold over the other half so it resembles a filled half-moon.

5. Grill for around 3 minutes on each side. Turn occasionally so that the tortilla doesn't burn.

6. Cut into slices, sprinkle with salt flakes, and serve warm, with Tabasco to taste.

1 sweet potato
salt
1 red chili pepper
7 oz (2 dl) mature cheese, grated
1 small can (7 oz / 198 g) corn
1 large bunch cilantro, chopped
4 large tortillas
salt flakes
Tabasco for serving

Watermelon Lemonade

4 servings

A refreshing drink for the barbeque. Feel free to mix in a drop of white rum to turn this lemonade into an icebreaker!

Directions

1. Peel and slice the melon into chunks.

2. Add the lemon juice and ice cubes and mix in a blender or food processor.

3. Strain through a fine sieve and serve immediately!

$2\frac{1}{4}$ lb (1 kg) watermelon
$\frac{1}{4}$ c ($\frac{1}{2}$ dl) freshly squeezed lemon juice
15 ice cubes

Beef Sandwich with Mustard Mayonnaise & Pickled Red Onion

4 servings

This mayonnaise, with the bite of mustard and horseradish, also works well with freshly grilled fish.

Directions

1. Whisk the egg yolk and vinegar in a bowl. Add the oil in a thin stream while whisking, until it becomes a thick mayonnaise.

2. Mix the mayonnaise with the mustard and horseradish. Season with salt to taste.

3. Peel and thinly slice the onion. Mix with sugar, vinegar, and salt.

Allow to stand for 15 minutes.

4. Season the steaks with salt and pepper and grill for about 3–5 minutes on each side. Brush the bread with oil and grill alongside the steak for the final minute.

5. Slice the steak and serve on the grilled bread with romaine, tomatoes, mustard mayonnaise, and pickled red onion.

4 steaks, 5.5 oz (150 g), e.g., sirloin

salt

freshly ground black pepper

sliced white sourdough bread

$\frac{1}{2}$ head romaine lettuce

9 oz (250 g) cherry tomatoes, sliced

Mustard mayonnaise

1 egg yolk

2 tsp white wine vinegar

$\frac{1}{2}$ c (1 dl) canola oil or other neutral-flavored vegetable oil

$\frac{1}{4}$ c ($\frac{1}{2}$ dl) coarse-grained mustard

salt

1 tbsp finely grated fresh horseradish

salt

Pickled red onion

2 red onions

1 tbsp sugar

2 tbsp white wine vinegar

$\frac{1}{5}$ tsp salt

Tomato Salad with Black Lentils

Sweet summer tomatoes with nutty black lentils combine in a salad with sharp lime and cilantro. This is a salad that goes with any barbeque.

Directions

1. Cook the lentils in plenty of salted water for around 20 minutes. Drain and rinse quickly under cold water.

2. Mix the lentils with tomato, onion, avocado, and olive oil. Add lime juice to taste, and season with salt and pepper. Add whole cilantro leaves and serve.

$\frac{4}{5}$ c (2 dl) beluga lentils

10.5 oz (300 g) cherry tomatoes, sliced

1 green onion, sliced

1 avocado, diced

2 tbsp olive oil

1 lime, squeezed

salt flakes

freshly ground black pepper

1 bunch fresh cilantro

Pickles and Piccalilli

Piccalilli is a spicy British pickle with mustard, coriander, cumin, and ginger. You can either make a classic Swedish pickle with dill and allspice, or piccalilli using the same vegetables.

Directions

1. Peel and thinly slice the carrots. Peel the onions and slice into thin wedges. Split the cauliflower into small florets. Dice the zucchini.

2. Cook the carrots in salted water for 5 minutes. When 1 minute remains add the onion and cauliflower. Drain and rinse under cold water.

3. Mix the vegetables in a heated pickling liquid of your choice (below). Store in clean glass jar and keep in a cool place.

4. For pickles: Heat the vinegar, sugar, water, allspice, and bay leaf. Mix in the dill and vegetables.

5. For piccalilli: Whisk the cornstarch, mustard powder, mustard seeds, turmeric, ginger, coriander, cumin, salt, and 1/2 cup vinegar. Heat the rest of the vinegar and whisk in the spice mix and sugar. Leave to simmer for 3 minutes.

Vegetables

6 carrots

2 yellow onions

1 cauliflower head

1 zucchini

Pickles

1 c (2 dl) vinegar essence (12 percent)

1 c (2 dl) sugar

3 c (6 dl) water

8 allspice corns

3 bay leaves

2 dill sprigs

Piccalilli

1 tbsp cornstarch

$1\frac{1}{2}$ tbsp Coleman's mustard powder

1 tsp brown mustard seeds

1 tsp turmeric

1 tsp ground ginger

1 tsp coriander seeds

1 tsp cumin seeds

1 tsp salt

$\frac{1}{2}$ c + 2 c (1 + 4 dl) apple cider vinegar

$\frac{1}{2}$ c (1 dl) sugar

Béarnaise Sauce

If the sauce separates, you can heat up a couple of tablespoons of cream or water in another pan. Gradually whisk the unsuccessful sauce into the cream/water and, hey presto! You have a lovely smooth Béarnaise sauce again.

Directions

1. Peel and finely chop the onion. Mix with water, vinegar, and tarragon in a saucepan.
2. Simmer uncovered over low heat for a couple of minutes.
3. In a separate pan, melt the butter, remove it from the heat, and allow the white protein to sink to the bottom of the pan.
4. Trickle the vinegar into the saucepan and whisk in the egg yolks over low heat until the eggs begin to coagulate.
5. Slowly add the butter in a thin stream while vigorously whisking into a thick sauce.
6. Add salt to taste.

1 shallot

$\frac{1}{2}$ tbsp white wine vinegar

2 tbsp water

2 tsp fresh tarragon, finely chopped

4 oz (100 g) butter

2 egg yolks

salt

Herby Ricotta Dip

Use cottage cheese or cream cheese if you don't have ricotta handy.

Directions

1. Mix the herbs and oil with a hand blender until smooth.
2. Fold in half of the herb oil with grated garlic, yogurt, and ricotta. Season with salt and pepper to taste.
3. Drizzle the rest of the herb oil over the dip when serving.

$\frac{2}{5}$ c (1 dl) basil, finely chopped

$\frac{2}{5}$ c (1 dl) parsley, finely chopped

$\frac{1}{5}$ c ($\frac{1}{2}$ dl) thyme, finely chopped

$\frac{1}{4}$ c ($\frac{1}{2}$ dl) olive oil

$\frac{1}{2}$ clove of garlic, grated

6.75 fl oz (2 dl) Turkish yogurt (or any plain yogurt)

9 oz (250 g) ricotta cheese

salt

freshly ground black pepper

Feta Cheese Dip
with Thyme and Lemon

4 servings

A creamy dip with the salty taste of sheep's cheese and tart lemon.

Directions

1. Crumble the feta cheese. Mix with the yogurt and the finely grated zest of half a lemon.
2. Add freshly squeezed lemon juice, salt, and pepper to taste.
3. Garnish the dip with herbs and grated lemon zest and drizzle with olive oil.

5.5 oz (150 g) feta cheese
$\frac{1}{2}$ c (1 dl) Turkish yogurt (or any plain yogurt)
1 lemon
salt
freshly ground black pepper
$\frac{1}{2}$ tbsp fresh thyme, finely chopped
$\frac{1}{2}$ tbsp parsley, finely chopped
1 tbsp olive oil

Romesco Sauce

4 servings

A splendid Spanish sauce — with the piquant taste of grilled peppers and almonds — that goes perfectly with grilled dishes.

Directions

1. Light the oven broiler to 475 degrees F (250 degrees C).
2. Deseed and slice the bell pepper. Halve the tomato. Spread the pepper and tomato, skin sides up, on a tray lined with parchment paper. Broil in the oven until the skins blacken.
3. Place the pepper and tomato in a bowl and cover with plastic wrap. Allow to cool then remove the skins.
4. Mix the pepper, tomato, garlic, almonds, vinegar, and oil with a hand blender or in a food processor.
5. Season with salt and vinegar to taste. Add more vinegar if required.

1 red bell pepper
1 tomato
1 garlic clove
1.75 oz (50 g) roasted almonds
1 tbsp red wine vinegar
$\frac{1}{4}$ c ($\frac{1}{2}$ dl) olive oil
salt
freshly ground black pepper

Raita

4 servings

A refreshing yogurt dip.

Directions

1. Peel and finely dice the cucumber.
2. Mix with grated garlic, mint, and yogurt. Add salt to taste.
3. Garnish the dip with cumin, olive oil, and pepper. Add mint leaves if desired.

$\frac{1}{2}$ cucumber
$\frac{1}{2}$ garlic clove, grated
2 tbsp fresh mint, finely chopped
+ whole leaves for garnishing
8.5 fl oz ($2\frac{1}{2}$ dl) Turkish yogurt (or any plain yogurt)
salt
$\frac{1}{5}$ tsp cumin seeds
olive oil
freshly ground black pepper

MUSIC TIPS

The Black Keys –
El Camino

For that moment
when you bury
4 six-packs of Bud
in a barrel of ice.

Tenderloin Kebab
with Indian Rub

4 servings

A rub is a spice mix massaged into the meat prior to grilling. The meat can be left to marinate in the spices overnight in the refrigerator. However, wait until directly before grilling to add salt, as it will draw out the moisture from the meat.

Directions

1. Dice the meat into ¾-inch cubes.
2. Grind the spices and sugar together with a mortar and pestle. Massage the spice mixture into the meat. Skewer the pieces immediately or leave overnight in the refrigerator to allow the meat to really absorb the flavors of the spices.
3. Immediately before grilling, season with salt and pepper and drizzle with olive oil.
4. Grill for around 10–15 minutes. Serve with refreshing raita (page 29) and sliced cucumber.

1 lb 12 oz (800 g) pork tenderloin

salt

freshly ground black pepper

olive oil

Indian rub:

1 tsp paprika

1 tsp curry powder

1 tsp coriander seeds

1 tsp cumin seeds

2 tsp muscovado sugar

Additional Rubs

BBQ rub

1 tsp cumin seeds

1 tsp smoked paprika

1 tsp anchovy powder

$\frac{1}{2}$ tsp freshly ground black pepper

1 tbsp dark muscovado sugar

Herb rub

1 tsp fennel seeds

1 tsp dried thyme

1 tsp dried rosemary

1 tsp oregano

$\frac{1}{2}$ tsp tarragon

$\frac{1}{2}$ tsp freshly ground black pepper

grated lemon zest

Panzanella Salad

A perfect Italian summertime salad. Sweet summer tomatoes with salty anchovies and capers. Serve with freshly grilled fish or meat and a cold glass of rosé wine!

Directions

1. Heat the oven to 450 degrees F (225 degrees C).

2. Cut the bread into cubes and toss with 1 tablespoon of oil and a little sea salt on a parchment paper–lined tray.

3. Roast in the middle of the oven for around 10 minutes. Turn occasionally so that the bread cooks evenly. Allow to cool.

4. Slice the tomatoes and peel and thinly slice the onion. Chop the anchovies.

5. Mix 3 tablespoons olive oil, vinegar, and grated garlic.

6. Toss the tomatoes, onions, anchovies, capers, olives, and croutons in the mixture. Season with salt and pepper to taste. Finally, garnish with whole basil leaves.

3 slices white sourdough bread

1 + 3 tbsp olive oil

salt flakes

1 lb 2 oz (500 g) cherry tomatoes

1 red onion

5 anchovies

$1\frac{1}{2}$ tbsp white balsamic vinegar

$\frac{1}{2}$ garlic clove, grated

3 tbsp capers

$\frac{3}{5}$ c ($1\frac{1}{2}$ dl) Kalamata olives

salt

freshly ground black pepper

1 bunch of basil

Grilled Herring with
New Potatoes and Pickled Cucumber

4 servings

A summer favorite! It can be difficult to grill herring directly on the grill. Buy a fish basket or mesh to lay on the grill to make it easier.

Directions

1. Mix buttermilk, mustard, and 3 tablespoons dill.

2. Clip off the dorsal fins from the herring fillets. Toss the herring in the mixture and allow to marinate for at least 15 minutes or preferably overnight.

3. Mix the vinegar essence, sugar, water, and 1 tablespoon of dill in a bowl. Thinly slice the cucumber and stir in, allowing to stand for at least 15 minutes.

4. Boil the potatoes in salted water.

5. Season the herring with salt and pepper and grill close together for around 3 minutes on each side.

6. Serve the freshly grilled herring on crispbread with sliced new potatoes, cucumber, and a dollop of sour cream. Garnish with a sprig of dill and lemon wedges.

$\frac{1}{2}$ c (1 dl) buttermilk
$\frac{1}{4}$ c ($\frac{1}{2}$ dl) coarse-grained mustard
3 + 1 tbsp dill, finely chopped
16 herring fillets
$\frac{1}{4}$ c ($\frac{1}{2}$ dl) vinegar essence (12 percent)
$\frac{1}{2}$ c (1 dl) sugar
$\frac{3}{4}$ c (1$\frac{1}{2}$ dl) water
1 cucumber
1 lb 12 oz (800 g) new potatoes
salt
freshly ground black pepper
crispbread
5 fl oz (1$\frac{1}{2}$ dl) sour cream
dill sprigs, if desired
lemon wedges, if desired

Grilled Salmon with an Apple & Lemon Glaze

4 servings

Whole grilled salmon is a great party dish. Grill indirectly but make sure that the skin gets crisp and tasty (and of course is descaled). The glaze should be brushed on toward the end of grilling; otherwise the sweet mixture can easily burn.

salt

freshly ground black pepper

$\frac{1}{5}$ c ($\frac{1}{2}$ dl) fresh dill, finely chopped

1 side of salmon (about 2.25 lb / 1 kg)

Directions

1. Season with salt and pepper and rub dill into the salmon. Grill indirectly for around 25 minutes.

2. If you want a really crispy skin on the salmon you can lay it over the coals for 5 minutes until it crisps up and browns. The salmon should have a core temperature of about 125 degrees F (50 degrees C).

3. Cook the apple juice, lemon juice, and honey for around 5 minutes. Allow to cool.

4. Brush the salmon with the glaze toward the end of the grilling time. Serve with the primeur salad.

More Glaze Ideas; Mix Without Cooking

Apple and lemon glaze

$\frac{1}{4}$ c ($\frac{1}{2}$ dl) apple juice concentrate

$\frac{1}{2}$ c (1 dl) lemon juice, freshly squeezed

$\frac{1}{4}$ c ($\frac{1}{2}$ dl) honey

BBQ glaze

3 tbsp tomato puree

3 tbsp honey

$1\frac{1}{2}$ tbsp Chinese soy sauce

1 tsp white wine vinegar

1 tbsp fresh ginger, grated

$\frac{1}{2}$ tsp ground cumin

$\frac{1}{2}$ tsp smoked paprika

$\frac{1}{2}$ tsp Tabasco, chipotle flavor

Thai glaze

3 tbsp Thai sweet chili sauce

1 tbsp red curry paste

1 tsp lime juice, freshly squeezed

1 tbsp honey

$\frac{1}{2}$ tbsp sesame oil

1 tbsp fresh ginger, grated

---

1 lb 12 oz (800 g) new potatoes

2 green onions, finely sliced

9 oz (250 g) fresh green asparagus

3.5 oz (100 g) butter

1 bunch radishes, halved

$\frac{1}{5}$ c ($\frac{1}{2}$ dl) dill, finely chopped

$\frac{1}{2}$ lemon, freshly squeezed

salt

freshly ground black pepper

Primeur Salad with Browned Butter

4 servings

Browned butter gives a fine nutty taste to the new potatoes.

Directions

1. Scrub and boil the potatoes to cook them. Slice the green onions.

2. Peel the asparagus if it's tough. Cook the asparagus in salted water for around 3 minutes. Drain, and blanch in cold water.

3. Melt the butter in a saucepan over medium heat. When the butter stops sizzling a fine foam will form on the surface. When the butter begins to smell like nutty toffee and you can see small brown specks in the foam it's time to remove it from the heat.

4. Let the butter stand for a few minutes so that the browned protein sinks to the bottom.

5. Mix the potatoes, onions, asparagus, radishes, and dill with the butter and freshly squeezed lemon juice. Season with salt and pepper.

Thai Kebabs

4-6 servings

Juicy skewers with ginger, red curry, soy sauce, and sesame.

Directions

1. Cut the chicken into suitably sized chunks for skewering.

2. Mix the marinade and allow the meat to marinate for around 30 minutes.

3. Skewer and grill for around 15 minutes until the chicken is cooked through. Serve with crispy noodle salad.

1 lb 12 oz (800 g) chicken thigh fillets

Marinade

1½ tbsp ginger, grated

1 garlic clove, grated

1 tbsp red curry paste

½ tbsp white wine vinegar

1 tsp sesame oil

2 tbsp Japanese soy sauce

Crispy Noodle Salad

4 servings

A tasty picnic salad that can be served with the Thai kebabs.

Directions

1. Cook the noodles in plenty of water according to the instructions on the package. When 30 seconds of cooking time remains, add the sugar snap peas. Drain, rinse in cold water, and drain in a colander.

2. Mix the noodles and peas with grated ginger, 2 tablespoons lime juice, sesame oil, and canola oil.

3. Add the bell pepper, cucumber, and green onions. Season with salt and pepper. Add more lime juice to taste.

4. Mix in whole cilantro leaves and garnish with chopped peanuts. Serve with lime wedges.

7 oz (200 g) glass noodles

5.5 oz (150 g) sugar snap peas

½ tbsp ginger, finely grated

juice of 2 limes

½ tsp sesame oil

1 tbsp canola oil

1 red bell pepper, sliced

½ cucumber, diced

2 green onions, sliced

salt

freshly ground black pepper

1 bunch fresh cilantro

⅖ c (1 dl) peanuts, chopped

Chorizo Skewers
with Chicken & Peppers

4-6 servings

Fresh grilled chorizo is fantastically tasty, juicy, and full of flavor. If you can't get hold of fresh chorizo then any other kind will do just fine.

Directions

1. Prepare the marinade.
2. Cut each chicken thigh into 3 pieces, just the right size for the skewer.
3. Marinate the chicken for about 10 minutes.
4. Halve the chorizo links.
5. Deseed and slice the bell peppers. Peel the onions and cut into wedges.
6. Thread the chicken, chorizo, and vegetables onto the skewers.
7. Grill for around 15 minutes turning occasionally. Check that the chicken is cooked thoroughly; if not, continue to grill! You can also grill the lemon halves. Serve the skewers with potato salad.

1 lb 5 oz (600 g) chicken thigh fillets
14 oz (400 g) fresh chorizo
2 bell peppers
2 red onions
lemons

Marinade

$\frac{1}{2}$ tbsp paprika, preferably Spanish smoked
1 pinch cayenne pepper
$\frac{1}{2}$ garlic clove, grated
1 tbsp olive oil
1 tsp salt
$\frac{1}{2}$ tsp freshly ground black pepper

Potato Salad
with Saffron Vinaigrette

4-6 servings

A saffron yellow salad reminiscent of paella. A good complement to all types of grilled food.

Directions

1. Scrub and cook the potatoes in salted water. Drain and halve the potatoes.
2. Mix the saffron and vinegar in a bowl. Whisk in the olive oil.
3. Toss the just-cooked potatoes in the dressing and season with salt and pepper to taste.
4. Slice green onions if desired and add to the salad along with sweet peas and parsley.
5. Deseed the bell peppers and cut into pieces. Grill the peppers together with the tasty Spanish chorizo skewers, and mix with the salad to serve.

2.25 lb (1 kg) new potatoes
a pinch (0.25 g) saffron
$2\frac{1}{2}$ tbsp apple cider vinegar
$\frac{1}{4}$ c ($\frac{1}{2}$ dl) olive oil
salt
freshly ground black pepper
3 green onions if desired
5.5 oz (150 g) sweet peas
$\frac{2}{5}$ c (1 dl) flat leaf parsley, finely chopped
2 bell peppers

Fish Skewers
with Chili & Cilantro

4-6 servings

The fish is skewered on lemongrass stalks — it doesn't provide much flavor, but boy does it look good!

Directions

1. Cut the fish into suitably sized pieces for threading onto the lemongrass.

2. Skewer the pieces on the lemongrass.

3. Finely chop the cilantro. Deseed and finely chop the chili pepper.

4. Mix the cilantro and chili with the juice of half a lime and the olive oil.

5. Brush the skewers with the marinade and season with salt and pepper.

6. Grill the skewers for 10 minutes until the fish is cooked through. Don't cook for too long or the fish will become dry and fall apart. Serve with lime and a slice of watermelon.

1 lb 2 oz (500 g) salmon fillets

1 lb 2 oz (500 g) cod, or other white fish

6-8 lemongrass stalks

1 bunch of cilantro

$\frac{1}{2}$ red chili pepper

2 limes

2 tbsp olive oil

salt

freshly ground black pepper

4-6 pieces of watermelon

Grilled Lamb Sirloin
with Creamy Potato Salad

4 servings

Homemade potato salad is quick to make. Buy readymade mayonnaise if you don't want to whisk up your own.

Directions

1. Boil the potatoes. Allow to cool.
2. Make the mayonnaise: Whisk the egg yolks and vinegar together in a bowl. Whisk in a thin stream of oil.
3. Mix the mayonnaise with crème fraiche, mustard, and dill. Fold in the potatoes, capers, and thinly sliced red onion. Season with salt and pepper and more vinegar if required.
4. Season the lamb fillets with salt and pepper. Grill for about 10–15 minutes.

2.25 lb (1 kg) new potatoes

Mayonnaise

1 egg yolk

2 tsp white wine vinegar

$\frac{1}{2}$ c (1 dl) canola oil

1 c (2 dl) crème fraiche

3 tbsp coarse-grained mustard

$\frac{1}{5}$ c ($\frac{1}{2}$ dl) dill, finely chopped

3 tbsp capers

1 red onion, thinly sliced

salt

freshly ground black pepper

1 lb 12 oz (800 g) lamb sirloin fillets

Asian Raw Vegetable Salad

4 servings

Crisp Swedish style root vegetables with an Asian dressing.

Directions

1. Toast sesame seeds in a dry, hot skillet. Allow to cool.
2. Peel and thinly slice the carrots and turnip. Shred or julienne the slices.
3. Deseed and finely chop the chilies. Mix with ginger, oil, soy sauce, lime juice, and chopped cilantro.
4. Toss the root vegetables in the dressing. Garnish with sesame seeds.

2 tbsp sesame seeds

$\frac{1}{2}$ turnip

2 carrots

$\frac{1}{2}$ red chili pepper

1 tbsp fresh ginger, grated

1 tbsp canola oil

$\frac{1}{2}$ tsp sesame oil

2 tbsp Japanese soy sauce

1 lime, freshly squeezed

1 bunch cilantro, chopped

Potato Gratin with Chanterelles and Kohlrabi

4 servings

You can use new potatoes for the gratin, but they may contain more water than regular potatoes. Use double cream and the gratin will be delightfully velvety.

Directions

1. Heat the oven to 400 degrees F (200 degrees C).

2. Peel and slice the potatoes and kohlrabi. Peel and thinly slice the onion.

3. Layer potatoes, kohlrabi, onions, and thyme in a buttered oven dish. Season with salt and pepper.

4. Pour on the cream and place the dish in the middle of the oven. Bake for 45 minutes.

5. Lightly sauté the chanterelles and scatter over the gratin before serving. Garnish with chopped thyme if desired.

1.5 lb (700 g) potatoes

10.5 oz (300 g) kohlrabi

1 yellow onion

1 tbsp fresh thyme, chopped + extra for garnishing

salt

freshly ground black pepper

$1\frac{1}{2}$ c (3 dl) double cream (or heavy cream, preferably fresh)

butter

10.5 oz (300 g) chanterelle mushrooms

CLASSIC BISTRO GRILL

Imagine a classic bistro, the prim & proper service, heavy velvet drapes, and traditional table settings. From the kitchen come uncomplicated dishes prepared with the very best ingredients, simple and delicious.

Liselotte Forslin

MENU

Grilled Meats

Veal Entrecôte

Lamb Chops

Fillet of Beef with Bacon

Sauces

Béarnaise

Café de Paris

Red Wine Sauce

Flavored Butters

Truffle Butter

Lemon Herb Butter with Anchovies Nut Butter

Side Dishes

Grilled Garlic

Heston's Potatoes

Salad with French Dressing

Tomato Gratin

Mushrooms à la Grecque

Marinated Haricots Verts

Veal Entrecôte

8 buffet servings

Veal is a real luxury of course, but be a conscious consumer. Ask your butcher where the meat is sourced and if it comes from free range animals.

Directions

1. Trim the meat to remove any sinew. Rub with salt, pepper, and dried herbs.

2. Grill on high heat, turning occasionally, until the meat achieves a good color.

3. Move the charcoal toward the edges so that the meat isn't directly over the coals. Put the lid on and finish grilling until you get a core temperature of 136–140 degrees F (58–60 degrees C). You could also leave the meat to finish cooking in the oven at 300 degrees F (150 degrees C).

4. Allow the meat to rest for 10 minutes before carving it into half-inch-thick slices. Season lightly with salt before serving.

5. Serve with lemon slices and fresh oregano sprigs.

2 lb 12 oz (1.2 kg) veal entrecôte, at room temperature

salt flakes

freshly ground black pepper

2-3 tbsp herbes de Provence

1 lemon, halved and sliced

$\frac{1}{2}$ bunch oregano

Lamb Chops

8 buffet servings

There's pretty much no meat that beats lamb chops on the grill. Delicious! Bear in mind that you'll get through quite a few as there isn't much meat on the bone. Serve with red wine sauce and truffle butter.

Directions

1. Brush the lamb chops with olive oil and grill for 3–4 minutes on each side.
2. Halve the lemon and grill with the cut edge down. Squeeze the juice over the chops.
3. Sprinkle over the herbs and garnish with a sprig of rosemary.
4. Season generously with salt and pepper.

24 lamb chops, at room temperature
$\frac{1}{4}$ c ($\frac{1}{2}$ dl) olive oil
1 lemon
3 tbsp parsley, chopped
3 tbsp rosemary, chopped
rosemary sprigs
salt
freshly ground black pepper

Grilled Garlic

8 buffet servings

Garlic has a very mild flavor if boiled lightly and then grilled on the cut edge. Serve the soft cloves on the side with meat, or on bread with a little olive oil and salt.

Directions

1. Boil the garlic for around 10 minutes in the skin.
2. Slice each head in half crosswise and brush the cut edges with olive oil. Grill quickly until it colors.
3. Season with salt and serve.

4 garlic heads
olive oil
salt flakes

Fillet of Beef with Bacon

8 buffet servings

This dish feels very '80s but hey, it's good! Bacon works well as the fillet of beef is lean and doesn't have a lot of flavor. Be careful that the meat isn't overcooked; to get the best out of fillet of beef it should be done medium rare.

Directions

1. Cut **8** generous portions of beef. Season generously with salt and pepper.

2. Wrap bacon around each and fasten with a cocktail stick.

3. Grill for about **3** minutes on each side.

2 lb 12 oz (1.2 kg) fillet of beef

salt flakes

freshly ground black pepper

approx. 8-10 slices bacon

small cocktail sticks

Clockwise from left: lemon herb
butter with anchovies, nut
butter, and truffle butter.

Truffle Butter

8 buffet servings

Invest in a slightly more expensive truffle oil than you usually find in the store; it's definitely worth the money. This butter is perfect with a steak, veal entrecôte, or beef fillet.

Directions

1. Sauté the mushrooms in butter and season with salt. Allow to cool.
2. Mix the mushrooms with the butter and stir in the truffle oil.
3. Roll the butter into a log in waxed paper or divide into small individual bowls, and refrigerate. Slice up the roll to serve.

2 large crimini mushrooms, finely chopped
2 tbsp butter
$\frac{1}{2}$ tsp salt flakes
7 oz (200 g) butter
1 tsp truffle oil

Lemon Herb Butter with Anchovies

8 buffet servings

This butter goes splendidly with lamb, veal, fish, or chicken.

Directions

1. Chop the anchovies, garlic, parsley, and thyme. Mix with the butter and lemon zest.
2. Roll the butter into a log in waxed paper or divide into small individual bowls, and refrigerate. Slice up the roll to serve.

5 anchovy fillets
1 garlic clove
$\frac{1}{2}$ bunch parsley
$\frac{1}{4}$ bunch thyme
7 oz (200 g) butter
1 tbsp lemon zest, grated

Nut Butter

8 buffet servings

Nut butter without any nuts! When you heat up butter precisely until it browns it creates a fantastic nutty taste. Prepare this a day in advance so it has time to filter and chill.

Directions

1. Heat the butter in a pan just until it becomes nut brown. Be careful that it doesn't burn.
2. Remove from the heat and pass through a coffee filter in a coffee funnel so that all the burnt milk proteins remain in the filter. Carefully stir the contents of the filter from time to time.
3. Divide into small individual bowls or egg cups. Cover with plastic wrap and chill.
4. Season lightly with salt flakes when serving.

7 oz (200 g) butter
salt flakes

Heston's Potatoes

8 buffet servings

These potatoes will be wonderfully crisp if you use the floury type and cook them like this.

4.5 lb (2 kg) floury potatoes, cut into wedges	
1 $\frac{1}{4}$ c (2.5 dl) olive oil	
salt flakes	
freshly ground black pepper	

Directions

1. Heat the oven to 350 degrees F (175 degrees C).

2. Rinse the potatoes and cut into wedges.

3. Boil for 20 minutes. Remove with a slotted spoon and drain on paper towels.

4. Heat oil in a roasting pan in the oven for 5 minutes.

5. Add the potatoes and toss. Allow the potatoes to roast slowly in the middle of the oven for around 1½ hours.

6. Season generously with salt and pepper to taste.

Salad with French Dressing

8 buffet servings

Madame Qricket in Provence taught me this simple and delicious dressing. It's so simple and works perfectly with delicate salad leaves. Mix the salad with the dressing right before serving to keep it crisp.

1 garlic clove	
2 tsp French mustard	
$\frac{1}{2}$ lemon, squeezed	
$\frac{1}{2}$ c (1 dl) olive oil	
salt flakes	
freshly ground black pepper	
5-7 oz (150-200 g) small mixed salad leaves	

Directions

1. Peel and grate the garlic clove into a large bowl.

2. Add mustard and lemon juice and whisk.

3. Whisk in the oil a drop at a time at first, then in a fine stream so that you get a creamy dressing. Add a pinch of salt and a few twists of the pepper grinder.

4. Dress the salad with clean hands and season with salt and pepper to taste. Serve immediately.

MUSIC TIPS

Gordon Lightfoot – Gord's Gold

Just as good as Neil Young and Bob Dylan but he hasn't been played to death. Canadian charcoal.

Clockwise from top: Béarnaise,
red wine sauce, and Café de Paris.

Béarnaise

8 buffet servings

Nothing competes with a good Bearny! But don't overdo it, just a dollop melted over the meat.

Directions

1. Melt the butter, pour into a spouted container, and set aside.
2. Put the chopped onion, tarragon leaves, vinegar, water, salt, and peppercorns in a stainless steel saucepan. Allow to boil until nearly all the liquid has evaporated. Remove from the heat.
3. Whisk the egg yolks and mix them into the onion mixture.
4. Add the butter one drop at a time then in a thin stream while whisking vigorously until you get a thick sauce. Do not return the saucepan to the heat. Serve the sauce cold or lukewarm.

10.5 oz (300 g) butter

$\frac{1}{2}$ yellow onion, finely chopped

2 sprigs of tarragon, scraped

$\frac{1}{4}$ c ($\frac{1}{2}$ dl) white wine vinegar

$\frac{1}{4}$ c ($\frac{1}{2}$ dl) water

$\frac{1}{5}$ tsp salt

8 white peppercorns, lightly crushed

6 egg yolks

Café de Paris

8 buffet servings

A spicier version of béarnaise with a distinct flavor of curry.

Directions

1. Follow the Béarnaise recipe.
2. Mix the other ingredients together and stir in.

2 anchovy fillets

1 garlic cloves, grated

2 tsp curry powder

1 tsp Worcestershire sauce

2 tsp French mustard

$\frac{1}{2}$ tsp cayenne pepper

Red Wine Sauce

8 buffet servings

Red wine sauce is a must have with grilled meats. It's great if you have both red wine sauce and a dollop of Béarnaise with the same dish.

Directions

1. Sauté the onion, carrot, and bacon in oil in a saucepan until they begin to color.
2. Add tomato puree and let it cook together while stirring for a few seconds.
3. Add stock, wine, and soy sauce and continue to cook, covered, until it reduces to approx. 2½ cups (5 dl).
4. Mix everything until smooth. Season with salt, pepper, and sugar to taste.
5. If desired, thicken with cornstarch according to the instructions on the package.
6. Add a knob of butter and allow to melt.

1 shallot, finely chopped

1 carrot, finely diced

1 bacon strip, chopped

2 tbsp olive oil

2 tbsp tomato puree

2 c (4 dl) dark meat stock

1 c (2 dl) red wine

2 tbsp soy sauce

2 tsp sugar

salt

freshly ground black pepper

3-4 tbsp cornstarch for thickening if required

2 tbsp butter

Tomato Gratin

8 buffet servings

A classic side dish that goes with any grilled meats.

Directions

1. Heat the oven to 450 degrees F (225 degrees C).

2. Cut the tomatoes in half horizontally (see photo). Scoop out the flesh and discard it. Lay the halves upside down on paper towels to drain.

3. Remove the crusts from the bread and crumble finely.

4. Peel the garlic cloves and lay them on a large chopping board. Add the anchovies and herbs and chop everything together. Mix with the capers, pine nuts, and bread crumbs.

5. Fill the tomatoes with the mixture. Drizzle with a little olive oil. Season lightly with salt and pepper.

6. Bake in the middle of the oven for 10—15 minutes until the tomatoes begin to color.

8 large tomatoes
2 slices (4 oz / 130 g) sourdough bread
3 garlic cloves
1 can anchovies, 1.5 oz / 45 g
$\frac{3}{5}$ c ($1\frac{1}{2}$) dl fresh herbs, e.g., oregano, parsley
$\frac{2}{5}$ c (1 dl) capers
3 tbsp pine nuts
2 tbsp olive oil
salt flakes
freshly ground black pepper

Marinated Haricots Verts

8 buffet servings

Haricots verts are a classic. Marinate them so they take on the wonderful flavors of garlic and lemon.

Directions

1. Boil the beans rapidly in lightly salted water for about 3 minutes. Blanch quickly in ice cold water and allow to drain.

2. While the beans are still warm mix them in a bowl with the red onion and garlic.

3. Mix lemon juice and olive oil, and toss together with the bean mixture. Add salt and pepper to taste.

10.5 oz (300 g) slender green beans
1 red onion, sliced
3 garlic cloves, chopped
$\frac{1}{2}$ lemon, squeezed
$\frac{1}{2}$ c (1 dl) olive oil
salt flakes
freshly ground black pepper

Mushrooms à la Grecque
8 buffet servings

Even better if you make it a day in advance to give the flavors time to develop.

Directions

1. Heat the oil in a large saucepan. Add the mushrooms, garlic, and spices and fry together without letting it color.

2. Add the tomato puree and stir until it begins to sizzle.

3. Add wine, water, thyme, and parsley and leave to simmer, covered, for 10 minutes.

4. Add lemon and sugar to taste and season with salt and pepper. Stir in the olive oil.

$\frac{1}{4}$ c ($\frac{1}{2}$ dl) olive oil

9 oz (250 g) crimini mushrooms, quartered

2 garlic cloves, chopped

3 bay leaves

1 cinnamon stick

10 white peppercorns

1 tbsp tomato puree

$\frac{1}{2}$ c (1 dl) dry white wine

$\frac{1}{2}$ c (1 dl) water

3 thyme sprigs, chopped

3 parsley sprigs, chopped

1 tbsp fresh lemon juice

1 tsp sugar

salt

freshly ground black pepper

$\frac{1}{2}$ c (1 dl) olive oil

FAMILY GRILL FEST

Get together with a few other families and enjoy this great buffet. There's something here to suit the tastes of the big'uns and the little'uns alike.

A barbeque buffet can be delicious and wonderfully inviting. Not everything has to be grilled of course. You can make a buffet of side dishes to complement the barbeque or mix it up with some salads, sauces, and other sides. The main thing is the good company, the warmth from the grill, and a cold drink in your hand. Most important of all, it's a great opportunity to hang out together. Ask your friends to bring along a side dish or something for the grill and the party will almost fix itself.

Everybody's welcome at this friendly Grill Fest!

Liselotte Forslin

MENU

Grilled Vegetables with Ranch Dip
Grilled Pizza
Chorizo Skewers with Creamy Potato Salad
Itty Bitty Burgers
Fajitas with Chicken Thigh Fillets and Guacamole
Grilled Pineapple with White Chocolate and Ginger Ice Cream

Grilled Vegetables
with Ranch Dip

Serve as a light bite while waiting for the grill or as a side dish. Ranch dip is also perfect served to the kids along with grilled vegetables.

Directions

1. Begin with the ranch dip: Mix mayonnaise and sour cream. Mix in the other ingredients, and refrigerate for 30 minutes.

2. Peel the carrots and parboil them for 3–4 minutes in lightly salted water. Drain and blanch in ice cold water.

3. Remove the lower dry parts from the asparagus. Cut the squash into slanted half-inch-thick pieces.

4. Brush the tomatoes and other vegetables with oil and grill, turning occasionally, until they get a nice color. Season with salt and serve on cocktail sticks with the ranch dip.

Ranch dip

1 c (2 dl) mayonnaise

1 c (2 dl) sour cream

3 tbsp chives, chopped

2 tbsp parsley, chopped

1 garlic clove, grated

$\frac{1}{2}$ tsp salt

$\frac{1}{5}$ tsp sugar

$\frac{1}{5}$ tsp freshly ground white pepper

Vegetables

9 oz (250 g) carrots

9 oz (250 g) asparagus

1 yellow squash

9 oz (250 g) cherry tomatoes

olive oil

salt flakes

cocktail sticks

Grilled Pizza

8 buffet servings

Grilling pizza is a bit tricky but you can get some great results. Make a few large ones and slice into pieces, or make small individual pizzas. They even taste good cold.

Directions

1. Dissolve the yeast in lukewarm water in the bowl of a stand mixer.

2. Add the sea salt and olive oil and mix until the yeast is completely dissolved.

3. Gradually add the flour. Using the dough hook attachment, let the mixer work the dough for 10 minutes.

4. Prepare the grill so that the charcoal is a fine gray and the embers red hot. Oil the cooking grill.

5. Knead the dough lightly and cut into 4 pieces. Roll out as thinly as possible.

6. Brush both sides of the pizza bases with oil.

7. Put one pizza at a time on the grill for 2–3 minutes, without the lid. Turn carefully.

8. Layer on your choices from the list of suggested toppings. Grill with lid on for another 3–4 minutes. Add the final topping after removing the pizza from the grill.

9. Drizzle with a little olive oil and season with salt and pepper.

Dough

- 1 oz (25 g) yeast
- $\frac{1}{4}$ c ($\frac{1}{2}$ dl) lukewarm water (98 degrees F / 37 degrees C)
- 1 tsp sea salt
- 1 tbsp olive oil
- $2\frac{2}{5}$ c (6 dl) flour

Topping Combo 1

- $\frac{1}{2}$ c (1 dl) red pesto
- 14 oz (400 g) mozzarella
- $\frac{1}{2}$ c (1 dl) grilled peppers in oil, in strips
- $\frac{1}{2}$ c (1 dl) sun dried tomatoes in oil, in strips
- olive oil
- salt flakes
- freshly ground black pepper

Final topping

- 7 oz (200 g) Italian salami or Parma ham
- 2 oz (50 g) arugula

Topping Combo 2

- 1 jar (14 oz / 400 g) tomato sauce, or use homemade
- 14 oz (400 g) mozzarella
- olive oil
- salt flakes
- freshly ground black pepper

Final topping

- 1 bunch of basil

A LITTLE TIP!

Prepare the dough the day before and store overnight in the refrigerator.

MUSIC TIPS

Neville Brothers – Yellow Moon

If there's not already a full moon for your barbeque, this album will soon fix that.

Chorizo Skewers
with Creamy Potato Salad

8 buffet servings / 4-8 skewers

Everybody loves a sausage on a stick.

Directions

1. Begin with the potato salad: Scrub and boil the potatoes. Cut the larger ones into pieces.

2. Parboil the beans in lightly salted water for 3 minutes. Blanch in ice cold water and slice longways. Mix the potatoes and beans but save a few beans for garnish.

3. Slice the green onions and add to the mix.

4. Mix the mayonnaise and crème fraiche, then stir in the vinegar and mustard. Dress the salad and season with salt and pepper to taste. Refrigerate for at least 2 hours or preferably overnight.

5. Make a bed of salad leaves (see photo), pile on the salad, and garnish with tomatoes and the rest of the beans.

6. Skewer: Cut the bell pepper in thick slices. Thread the chorizo and peppers on 8 small or 4 large skewers and grill on medium heat for 6–8 minutes, turning occasionally.

Potato salad

1.5 lb (700 g) new potatoes
5 oz (150 g) fresh green beans
6 green onions
1 c (2 dl) mayonnaise
$\frac{1}{2}$ c (1 dl) crème fraiche
3 tbsp apple cider vinegar
2 tbsp strong sweet mustard
salt
freshly ground black pepper
1 head of lettuce, e.g. lollo rosso
3.5 oz (100 g) cherry tomatoes, halved

Skewer

1 yellow bell pepper
about 20 mini chorizo sausages
grill skewers

Itty Bitty Burgers

8 buffet portions / 16 burgers

Mini burgers that are exceedingly tasty, for big mouths and small.

Directions

1. Start with the mayonnaise: Mix the egg yolks, mustard, lemon juice, and salt in a large, wide bowl with a balloon whisk. When this is done begin to add the oil at first a drop at a time and then in a thin stream while whisking vigorously to trap air in the mixture. When the mayonnaise begins to thicken you can add a little thicker stream of oil.

2. Burgers: Mix the ground beef with barbeque sauce, salt, and pepper. Form into 16 burgers about the size of an apricot.

3. Cut out circles of bread using a small glass, about 2 inches in diameter. Toast the bread lightly on the grill or in the oven or toaster.

4. Rinse and dry the lettuce leaves and halve the tomatoes.

5. Grill the burgers for around 3 minutes on each side. Brush with a little barbeque sauce toward the end of the cooking time.

6. Place lettuce on the bread, dollop on a little mayonnaise and put the burger on top, then add another dollop of mayonnaise on top of that. Put a tomato onto each skewer and thread on the burger and bread. Garnish with a little oregano and season lightly with salt and pepper.

Mayonnaise

2 egg yolks

2 tsp French mustard

1 tbsp lemon juice

$\frac{1}{5}$ tsp salt

$\frac{1}{2}$ c (1 dl) canola oil, not cold pressed

$\frac{1}{2}$ c (1 dl) olive oil, cold pressed

Burgers

2.25 lb (1 kg) ground beef

$\frac{1}{2}$ c (1 dl) smoky barbeque sauce + extra to glaze

2 tsp salt

2 tsp freshly ground black pepper

16 slices white farmhouse bread, good quality

1 head loose leaf lettuce

8 cherry tomatoes

16 wooden grill skewers or cocktail sticks

fresh oregano

MUSIC TIPS

John Denver – Greatest Hits

The most enduring campfire sing-along songs are, and always will be, "Take Me Home, Country Roads" and "Leaving on a Jet Plane."

Fajitas with Chicken Thigh Fillets & Guacamole

8 buffet servings

It's so gratifying to fill your own tortilla and enjoy a spicy fajita.

Directions

1. Rinse the chicken and dry with paper towels. Mix the ingredients for the rub and massage the spice mixture into the chicken. Allow to stand in a plastic bag in the refrigerator for at least 1 hour.

2. Halve, deseed, and slice the bell peppers. Peel the red onion and cut into wedges. Set aside.

3. Guacamole: Halve the avocadoes and remove the pits, scoop out the flesh, and place in a bowl. Halve, deseed, and dice the tomato and chili. Peel the onion and finely chop. Finely grate the garlic cloves. Mix everything with the avocado flesh and squeeze in the lime juice. Chop the cilantro and mix in, then season with salt and pepper to taste. Garnish with lime wedges to serve.

4. Prepare the grill so the charcoal is a fine gray and the embers are red hot. Grill the chicken thigh fillets for around 8 minutes on each side and then shred.

5. Quickly grill the pepper and onion wedges, on a skewer or in a grill basket. Toss the chicken and vegetables together on a serving plate and garnish with oregano.

6. Warm the tortillas quickly on the grill. Let everyone fill his or her own tortilla and top off with guacamole.

8 chicken thigh fillets

Spice rub

1 tsp ground cumin

1 tsp Spanish smoked paprika

2 tsp salt flakes

Fajitas

1 yellow bell pepper

1 red bell pepper

1 large red onion

$\frac{1}{2}$ bunch oregano

small tortillas

Guacamole

2 large, ripe avocadoes

1 large tomato

1 red chili

$\frac{1}{2}$ yellow onion

2 garlic cloves

1 lime, freshly squeezed + lime wedges

1 bunch cilantro

1 tsp salt flakes

Grilled Pineapple with White Chocolate & Ginger Ice Cream

8 servings

A simple, delicious, and refreshing ice cream after all that grilled food.

Directions

1. Begin with the ice cream: Allow to defrost until it softens. While you're waiting, finely chop the chocolate. Mix the ginger and chocolate into the ice cream and freeze for 4–5 hours in a nice mold.

2. Cut the pineapple into 8 wedges. Brush lightly with the olive oil and grill for 3–4 minutes on each side.

3. Cut the lime into wedges. Dip the ice cream mold in hot water to loosen, and tip out the ice cream onto a plate.

4. Arrange the grilled pineapple and lime wedges around the sides. Let everyone squeeze their own lime over the pineapple.

$\frac{1}{2}$ gallon (2 l) vanilla ice cream, good quality

3.5 oz (100 g) white chocolate, finely chopped

2 tbsp ground ginger

1 pineapple

2 tbsp canola or other neutral-flavored vegetable oil

2 limes

MUSIC
TIPS

Ann Peebles –
I Can't Stand the
Rain

In one of the most
beautiful soul
songs of all time,
the magnificent
Ann Peebles sings,
"You got to feed
the fire, to make
the flame of love
grow higher."
Words for a grill
master to live by.

MEDITERRANEAN GRILL

A flirtation with the tastes of the Mediterranean and, especially, Italy. Enjoy this food with the salt air of a sun-kissed beach.
Liselotte Forslin

MENU

Grilled Souvlaki with Pork Tenderloin, Italian Sausage, and Rosemary

Grilled Eggplant, Squash, Mint, and Pomegranate Salad

Two Flavors of Focaccia

Grilled Bell Pepper Soup and Crostini with Tapenade

Grilled Mussels in Chili and Mint Vinaigrette

Grilled Peaches with Mozzarella, Red Onion, and Olives

Grilled Souvlaki
with Pork Tenderloin,
Italian Sausage, & Rosemary

8 buffet servings

The grilled orange plus the fennel in the Italian sausage gives an excellent flavor to the pork. You could even replace the pork with lamb or chicken.

Directions

1. Cut the meat into small pieces.

2. Cut the squash into half-inch-thick pieces then halve again.

3. Separate the rosemary sprigs or wooden skewers and brush with a little oil. Season lightly with salt and pepper.

4. Grill gently over medium heat so that the sausage is cooked through, about 6–7 minutes, turning occasionally. When the meat begins to color push the coals out to the edges of the grill and put the lid on so the food grills indirectly. Make a cut in the sausage to make sure it's done.

5. Quarter the orange and grill the cut edges. Squeeze the juice over the skewers when they are done.

1 pork tenderloin, about 1.5-1.75 lb (700-800 g)
10.5 oz (300 g) Italian raw sausage, preferably with fennel
1 squash
8 thick rosemary sprigs, or 8 soaked wooden skewers
olive oil
salt flakes
freshly ground black pepper
1 orange

Grilled Eggplant, Squash,
Mint, & Pomegranate Salad

8 buffet servings

There's just nothing better than grilled vegetables. They take on a light, smoky flavor that suits grilled meat perfectly.

Directions

1. Slice the vegetables diagonally in half-inch-thick slices so you get oval slices.

2. Brush lightly with oil and grill for a couple of minutes on each side so the vegetables achieve a nice color. Put them in a bowl.

3. Crumble the feta cheese over the bowl, and add the pomegranate seeds, saving a few seeds for garnishing.

4. Tear some mint leaves and add, saving some whole leaves for garnishing.

5. Mix in olive oil and lemon juice and season generously with salt and pepper.

6. Dish up the salad on a serving plate, and garnish with pomegranate seeds and mint leaves. Serve warm.

2 eggplants
2 zucchini squashes
olive oil
5.5 oz (150 g) feta cheese
1 pomegranate
1 small bunch of mint
3 tbsp olive oil
1 tbsp lemon juice
salt flakes
freshly ground black pepper

Two Flavors of Focaccia

8 buffet servings

A thin Italian bread with a tasty topping is just what any grill buffet needs. Serve fresh from the oven.

Directions

1. Heat the oven to 435 degrees F (225 degrees C).

2. Dissolve the yeast in tepid water in a bowl, preferably in a stand mixer with dough hook attachment.

3. Add salt and olive oil to the completely-dissolved yeast.

4. Add the flour little by little and allow the mixer to work the dough for 10 minutes until it comes away from the sides of the bowl.

5. Leave to rise for 30 minutes under a clean dish towel in a draft free place.

6. Lightly knead the dough and divide into 2 pieces. Roll, press out and form into 2 oblong bases. Place them on a baking tray.

7. Use your fingers to make small depressions in the dough. Place tomatoes, on the vine, on one and olives and raisins on the other. Drizzle with a little olive oil and sprinkle lightly with salt flakes.

8. Bake for about 10–12 minutes until the bread achieves a nice color. Remember that raisins burn easily so you may need a sheet of aluminum foil close by to lay over the foccacia while it bakes.

1 oz (25 g) yeast

$1\frac{1}{4}$ c ($2\frac{1}{2}$ dl) water (98 degrees F / 37 degrees C)

1 tsp salt

1 tbsp olive oil

$2\frac{2}{5}$ c (6 dl) flour

9 oz (250 g) vine tomatoes

$\frac{2}{5}$ c (1 dl) small black olives, good quality, without pits

$\frac{2}{5}$ c (1 dl) golden raisins

olive oil

salt

Grilled Bell Pepper Soup

8 small glasses

Personally I like to make two batches while I'm at it, one red and one yellow. It looks so pretty on the table. Serve in a small glass as an appetizer, accompanied by crostini and tapenade.

Directions

1. Grill the bell peppers on all sides until they blacken. Alternatively grill them in the oven at 525 degrees F (275 degrees C), first halving them, removing the seeds, and slicing them in quarters. Lay them on an oven tray lined with parchment paper, skin side up, and grill at the top of the oven. After 12–15 minutes the skin should be black.

2. Put the grilled peppers in a bowl with a lid for 20 minutes. Take off the lid and peel off the blackened skin. Remove the seeds if you grilled the peppers whole on the barbeque.

3. Slice the peppers. Peel and chop the onions and garlic.

4. Heat the oil in a large saucepan and fry the onions and garlic gently without allowing them to color. Add the bell pepper strips and pour in the wine. Allow to cook for a few minutes and then add the stock. Allow to simmer uncovered for 5 minutes.

5. Blend until smooth, and season with salt and pepper. Serve warm or cold drizzled with a little olive oil.

Ingredients
6 bell peppers, red or yellow
1 yellow onion
2 garlic cloves
$\frac{1}{4}$ c ($\frac{1}{2}$ dl) olive oil
1 c (2 dl) white wine vinegar
$3\frac{1}{2}$ c (7 dl) chicken stock
salt flakes
freshly ground black pepper
olive oil for serving

Crostini with Tapenade

10-12 buffet servings

Directions

1. Put the olives, garlic, anchovies, and capers into a mixer and blend until smooth.

2. Add olive oil and blend until it's mixed in.

3. Season with salt and pepper to taste.

4. Grill or toast the bread slices in the oven at 425 degrees F (225 degrees C). Serve the crostini with tapenade alongside the soup.

Ingredients
7 oz (200 g) Kalamata olives, pits removed
2 garlic cloves
5 anchovy fillets
3 tbsp capers
$\frac{1}{2}$ c (1 dl) olive oil
salt
freshly ground black pepper
1 baguette, sliced

A LITTLE TIP!

Pour the soup into rinsed-out soda or water bottles and take them with you to your barbeque on the beach.

MUSIC
TIPS

Tinariwen –
Tassili

A campfire lit
in the desert.
Hypnotic,
acoustic,
slow burning
Sahara blues.

Grilled Mussels in Chili and Mint Vinaigrette

8 buffet servings

Grilling mussels is actually easier than cooking them with other methods. Just wrap them in foil with a dash of white wine. Afterwards marinate them in a vinaigrette with a bit of devilish spice in it. You can serve them right away or refrigerate for later.

Directions

1. Mix all of the ingredients for the marinade.

2. Rinse and debeard the mussels. Any mussels that are open and don't close when tapped on a hard surface are dead and should be thrown away. This also applies to any broken ones.

3. Lay out two large double sheets of foil on top of each other and pile the mussels in the middle. Make into a packet, add the wine, and seal well. You could make two smaller packets if you prefer.

4. Place the packet on the grill and cover with the lid. Grill for around 6–7 minutes, until the mussels open.

5. Place the mussels and broth in a bowl and pour on the vinaigrette. Serve at room temperature or cold.

Vinaigrette

$\frac{3}{4}$ c ($1\frac{1}{2}$ dl) olive oil

1 lemon, squeezed

2/5 c (1 dl) flat leaf parsley, chopped

2-3 red chili peppers, chopped

garlic cloves, chopped

$\frac{1}{2}$ tsp salt

4.5 lb (2 kg) blue mussels

$\frac{1}{2}$ c (1 dl) white wine

Grilled Peaches with
Mozzarella, Red Onion, & Olives

8 buffet servings

It's a real treat to grill peaches when they're in season. This is almost like a dessert but the red onion, olives, and balsamic vinegar turn it into a side dish or a starter. Best served straight from the grill.

Directions

1. Halve the peaches, remove the pits, and cut into half-inch-thick slices.

2. Brush lightly with olive oil on both sides and grill rapidly to achieve a nice grill pattern.

3. Place the peach slices on a plate. Tear up the mozzarella and scatter it over, along with the red onion slices.

4. Spread the olives over and sprinkle with salt flakes. Do a couple of laps around the plate with the pepper mill.

5. Mix together the oil, balsamic vinegar, and honey and spoon over. Serve lukewarm or at room temperature (but not chilled).

8 peaches, white-flesh or ordinary

Olive oil for grilling

14 oz (400 g) mozzarella

1 red onion, thinly sliced

2/5 c (1 dl) small black olives with pits, good quality

salt flakes

freshly ground black pepper

$\frac{1}{4}$ c ($\frac{1}{2}$ dl) olive oil

2 tbsp balsamic vinegar

2 tsp honey

BBQ SWEDISH STYLE

The most delicious thing I ever tasted in the way of grilled food was a mouthful of BBQ brisket from a small, blue painted shack at a sweltering gas station in Austin, Texas. With smoke puffing from its tin stack and steam spreading and mingling with the scorching heat of the day, it was so utterly hypnotic I was drawn, as if bewitched, toward the service window. We were en route to what promised to be a real feast, and food should have been the last thing on my mind, but they gladly offered me a taste free of charge. It was as if, from the very first bite, the world stood still. The meat veritably melting in the mouth, those tarry, smoky flavors, dark, tart, juicy, and so insanely delicious.

BBQ, or barbeque if you prefer, is an American championship sport. In Texas they bury their joint of meat in a pit in the backyard and let it simmer and smoke and do its thing for eight hours. With the right music coming from the speakers, of course. We don't really go in for that in Sweden. Charming as it is, it seems a bit impractical. When I made my mind up a few years ago that it was time for a bit of Girl Power around the barbeque, I quickly realized that the rules are there to be broken. All you need is intuition and self-confidence. And quality meat.

That's to say, I'm not afraid to cheat. I'll use any trick, buckets, bottles, canned goods, anything I can get my hands on to find a shortcut back to that sweltering gas station in Austin. Barbeque is all about drawing out those seductive charcoal-tinged, smoky flavors. I may not have a grill pit, or even a backyard to put one in, but I'll do it my way. A BBQ Swedish style, with an unbeatable soundtrack? It might not be perfect, but it's near enough.

Mia Gahne

Martini Blush

1 glass

My slightly gentler version of a dry martini — just made for sipping around the grill.

Directions

1. Fill a martini glass with ice.

2. Mix gin, vermouth, Campari, and lime juice in a shaker. Add more ice and shake. Taste.

3. Throw away the ice in the glass. Sieve and pour into the glass. Garnish with a sprig of mint or a slice of lime.

ice
1.5 oz (4 cl) gin
$\frac{1}{3}$ oz (1 cl) dry vermouth
$\frac{2}{3}$ oz (2 cl) Campari
1 lime
1 mint sprig or lime slice

Smoky Mary

1 glass

An awesome variation on the classic Bloody Mary. Bloody Mary mix should be available in supermarkets, but can be replaced with ordinary tomato juice.

Directions

1. Pour a measure of vodka into a tumbler.

2. Add Mr. & Mrs. T or tomato juice, lemon cordial, Worcestershire sauce, liquid smoke, and Tabasco to taste. Fill up with ice. Add herb salt, black pepper, and extra lemon cordial to taste.

3. Garnish with a stalk of celery and serve.

1.5 oz (4 cl) vodka
$\frac{3}{4}$ c (1$\frac{1}{2}$ dl) Mr. & Mrs. T Bloody Mary Mix, or alternatively tomato juice
1.5 oz (4 cl) lemon cordial
$\frac{1}{3}$ oz (1 cl) Worcestershire sauce
$\frac{1}{3}$ oz (1 cl) liquid smoke
a few drops Tabasco, preferably chipotle flavor
ice
herb salt
freshly ground black pepper
1 celery stalk

MUSIC TIPS

Ray Charles – Modern Sound in Country & Western Music

Anyone who doesn't feel like having a cocktail after hearing a song like "Half as Much" will probably never feel like having a cocktail!

MUSIC TIPS

Dr. John – Gris Gris

Gris may mean pig in Swedish, but I don't think that's what Dr. John had in mind. Still, the rhythms he's rolling out are hot as burning coals. "I walk on gilded splinters."

Black Bean Salad

4 servings

Black beans are commonly found in both salads and soups in the South. They have a lovely sweetness that goes perfectly with grilled food. A fresh and tasty bean salad always hits the spot . . .

Directions

1. Rinse the beans and drain thoroughly. Pour into a bowl.
2. Press lime juice over the red onions. Allow to stand for 10 minutes. Add salt, cumin, cinnamon, honey, and olive oil. Taste and adjust seasonings.
3. Halve the tomatoes.
4. Carefully mix the beans, tomatoes, peppers, chili, and cilantro. Pour over the dressing and toss lightly.
5. Serve with, for example, grilled pork.

1 can (15 oz / 425 g) black beans

1 lime

2 small red onions, sliced and sprinkled with salt

1 tsp ground cumin

$\frac{1}{2}$ tsp cinnamon

$\frac{1}{2}$ tsp honey

3 tbsp olive oil

4 cherry tomatoes

1 orange bell pepper, deseeded and sliced

1 red chili pepper, deseeded and finely chopped

1 bunch fresh cilantro, roughly chopped

Grilled Cinnamon Pork

4 servings

Post beach hunger and a verging-on-empty meat counter saw the creation of this dish — which soon became a quick 'n' lazy, tasty summer favorite.

Directions

1. Spread the pork slices out on the counter or chopping board.
2. Mix all the spices and sugar in a small bowl. Sprinkle half of the spice mix on the pork slices then turn them over and sprinkle the rest on the other side. Massage the spices thoroughly into the meat.
3. Grill on a really hot grill with direct heat for a couple of minutes on each side. Serve right away. Goes well with iceberg slaw (page 105) or the bean salad above.

about 1 lb 2 oz (500 g) smoked pork belly or slab bacon, sliced

2 tsp cinnamon

1 tsp ground coriander

2 tsp smoked paprika

1 tsp oregano

1 tsp ground ginger

1 tsp cayenne pepper

2 tbsp brown sugar

Chipotle Fishcakes

Asia meets America in these really simple, quick and delicious fishcakes. Oil the grill liberally or use a fish basket.

Directions

1. Dry the fish thoroughly and blend quickly in a food processor, or chop by hand.

2. Pour the fish into a bowl and mix with curry paste, chipotle paste, egg, and green beans.

3. Fold the lime leaves and pull off the stalks. Finely chop the rest and mix into the fishcake mix along with the salt and sugar.

4. Mix the ingredients for the dipping sauce and taste. Adjust seasonings as needed.

5. Form the fish mixture into cakes. Brush with oil and grill for a couple of minutes on each side.

6. Serve with lime wedges and dipping sauce.

1 lb 2 oz (500 g) white fish, e.g., haddock, cod

1 tbsp red curry paste

about $\frac{1}{2}$ tsp chipotle paste

1 egg

2/5 c (1 dl) green beans, finely sliced

10 lime leaves

1 tsp salt

1 tsp sugar

oil

limes

Dipping sauce

1 lime, juice only

1 tbsp sesame oil

2 tbsp canola oil

2 tbsp sweet chili sauce

about 1 tsp chipotle paste

1 tbsp fish sauce

Smoky Sirloin

Whole grilled fillet of beef is a practical and delicious dish to impress your guests with. Be careful that the meat doesn't get too dry. Juicy, smoky, and full of flavor, that's what you want. Serve with chipotle aioli.

Directions

1. Trim the beef and pat dry with paper towels.

2. Crush the garlic cloves with the flat of the knife blade. Chop finely with a pinch of salt until you get a creamy paste. Pour the garlic into a bowl and add paprika, cumin, pepper, and olive oil. Blend well.

3. Massage the mixture thoroughly into the meat and allow to rest while the grill heats up. Fold the thin part (if there is one) underneath and tie with string so that the meat is evenly thick. Stick a meat thermometer in the middle.

4. Brown the meat on all sides on the grill over direct heat, then move the meat to an indirect heat outside the coals. Put the lid on and grill until the inner temperature reaches 130–140 degrees F (55–60 degrees C), according to taste.

5. Place the meat on a plate and allow to rest for 10 minutes.

6. Carve into slices and serve with chipotle aioli, smoky sesame spuds (see recipe on page 105), and steamed vegetables.

about 3 lb 5 oz (1½ kg) whole fillet of beef
5 garlic cloves
salt
2 tbsp mild smoked paprika
1 tbsp cumin
freshly ground black pepper
3 tbsp olive oil

Chipotle Aioli

4 servings

With a little patience you can create a superb smoky, slightly hot aioli that goes well with anything grilled but is especially fantastic with shellfish and burgers. Make sure that all the ingredients are at the same temperature. Of course, if you like you can cheat with ready-made mayonnaise but the results won't be half as great.

Directions

1. Mix egg yolks, garlic, lime juice, salt, and bread or potato.

2. Add the oil, a drop at a time to begin with, while whisking vigorously (an electric whisk is great for this!). After a while you can add the oil in a thin stream but don't stop whisking until the aioli is thick and smooth (use as much oil as you need to achieve the correct taste and consistency).

3. Add the chipotle and a few drops of liquid smoke if desired. Mix quickly. Add salt and maybe a little lemon juice to taste.

2 egg yolks
2 garlic cloves, grated
½ to 1 tsp lime juice
½ tsp salt
1 slice dry white bread or 1 boiled potato
about ¾ c (1½ dl) vegetable oil
about ½ c (1 dl) mild olive oil or cold pressed canola oil
1 tsp chipotle paste or blended chipotle in adobo
½ tsp liquid smoke, optional
lemon juice, optional

MIA'S SMOKIN' TIPS & TRICKS

CHIPOTLE – smoked jalapeno chilies. If you see anything in the store that says chipotle on it, buy it. It gives the perfect smoky flavor with just the right amount of heat. These days on the taco shelf you can find chipotle paste. This is fine but the absolute best is chipotle in adobo: chipotle preserved in a magical sauce. It's perfectly OK to freeze after opening, and then you can take it out and carve off a slice the next time you grill. Dried chipotle needs to be soaked.

PIMENTÓN DE LA VERA – Spanish smoked paprika. Available as hot (picante) or mild (dulce). Gives a wonderful, deep, smoky flavor. Goes well with almost anything that can be grilled. Available in all well-stocked markets. Seriously addictive.

LIQUID SMOKE – bottled smoke extract. You won't find much more of a cheat than this but it works. Perfect when preparing ribs for the barbeque. Use judiciously. Too much and it will just taste of chemicals, which is what it probably is.

SMOKING CHIPS – hickory or mesquite. Sling these on the fire for a deeper smoke flavor.

LAPSANG SOUCHONG – smoked tea. Brew and allow to stand and infuse for at least a couple of hours. After that you can use it as a flavoring in, for example, marinades and dressings. Taste your way so you don't overdo it.

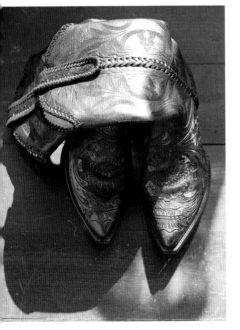

Pork Chops with Rhubarb Salsa

4 servings

There's not much that beats a grilled pork chop. Try and find them on the bone —
they're juicier and have more flavor. With this traditional Swedish salsa it'll be a
Swedish American megahit.

Directions

1. Make a cut in the fat at the edge of each chop and pat them dry.

2. Mix all the spices, lime zest, garlic, sugar, salt, and pepper. Add olive oil and stir
   into a thick paste. Massage the paste thoroughly into the meat. Allow to stand
   for at least 20 minutes. The marinated chops can be stored in a plastic bag in
   the refrigerator for up to 4 hours but remember that they should be at room
   temperature when you put them on the grill.

3. Use this time to make the salsa: Slice the rhubarb (peel it if it's tough). Mix the
   sesame oil, olive oil, chili, mint, honey, and sesame seeds and add. Mix in the
   ginger and red onion. Add salt to taste. You can even cook the salsa for 10
   minutes, but in that case add the mint after cooking.

4. Place the chops on the grill over direct heat and allow them to color on both
   sides. Move to the edge of the coals and put the lid on. Grill until an inner
   temperature of 145 degrees F (63 degrees C) is reached. Place on a serving
   plate and allow to rest for 5 minutes.

5. Serve with the salsa and why not try them with smoky sesame spuds (see page
   105).

4 large pork chops on the bone

2 tbsp mild paprika, preferably
smoked

$1\frac{1}{2}$ tbsp oregano

2 tsp cumin

$1\frac{1}{2}$ tsp chili powder, preferably
ancho

1 lime, grated zest

3 garlic cloves, finely chopped

2 tbsp brown sugar

salt flakes

freshly ground black pepper

$\frac{1}{4}$ c ($\frac{1}{2}$ dl) olive oil

Rhubarb salsa

5.25 oz (150 g) rhubarb

2 tsp sesame oil

$\frac{1}{4}$ c ($\frac{1}{2}$ dl) olive oil

$\frac{1}{2}$ red chili, sliced

2 tbsp mint, chopped

1-2 tbsp acacia honey

1 tbsp sesame seeds

$\frac{1}{5}$ c ($\frac{1}{2}$ dl) pickled ginger,
chopped

$\frac{1}{2}$ red onion, thinly sliced

salt

MUSIC
TIPS

Billie Holiday –
Lady Sings the
Blues

Makes you feel
like cancelling
the party and
grilling on
your own.

Spicy Pepper Chicken Wings

4 servings

Finger food is good food. These chicken wings make great mingle food. Don't be stingy with the pepper.

Directions

1. Wash the lemons and grate the zest. Peel the garlic cloves. Crush the lemon zest, garlic, bay leaves, peppercorns, paprika, and chili flakes with a mortar and pestle or process quickly in a food processor. The peppercorns should remain quite coarse.

2. Add olive oil and the juice from one lemon. Massage thoroughly into the wings. Allow to stand for 30 minutes. Sprinkle with salt flakes.

3. Spread the chicken wings out evenly on the grill or an oiled cooking basket. Grill over direct heat until the wings get color on all sides then move to indirect heat and put the lid on. Grill for 5 more minutes.

4. Eat with your fingers!

2 lemons
5 garlic cloves
10 bay leaves
1 tbsp black pepper corns
2-3 tsp mild smoked paprika
$\frac{1}{2}$ tsp chili flakes
$\frac{1}{4}$ c ($\frac{1}{2}$ dl) olive oil
2 lb 3 oz (1 kg) chicken wings
salt flakes, preferably smoked

Iceberg Slaw

4 servings

Just the thing to serve with barbeque ribs, for example. Don't be afraid to use the Aromat, a seasoning blend unusual in the US but available at some markets or online. It really makes the dish.

Directions

1. Shred the lettuce and green onions, saving the green portions of the onion stalks. Deseed the bell pepper and slice. Put all the vegetables into a bowl.

2. Mix sour cream, Aromat, and lemon juice. Pour the dressing over the salad and toss well. Garnish with the shredded onion stalks, parsley, and pea shoots.

about 12 oz (350 g) iceberg lettuce
2 green onions
1 orange bell pepper
1 c (2 dl) sour cream
1-2 tbsp Aromat
1 tsp lemon juice
2 tbsp flat leaf parsley
pea shoots

Smoky Sesame Spuds

4 servings

Give new potatoes a little smoky flavor. A nice side dish that goes with anything.

Directions

1. Scrub the potatoes and boil them until almost done, about 5–10 minutes, depending on their size and freshness. Drain and allow to cool somewhat.

2. Put the potatoes in a double plastic bag. Add canola oil, sesame oil, liquid smoke, paprika, and sesame seeds. Mix thoroughly. Allow to stand while you prepare the grill.

3. Take the potatoes out of the bag, drain, and season with salt flakes. You can also thread the potatoes onto skewers (presoaked if they're wood). Grill until the potatoes are soft and have achieved a nice color. Serve with meat or fish.

2 lb 3 oz (1 kg) new potatoes
2 tbsp canola oil
2 tsp sesame oil
1 tsp liquid smoke
1 tsp smoked paprika
2/5 c (1 dl) sesame seeds
salt flakes, preferably smoked

MUSIC
TIPS

Barbeque Bob –
Blues Essentials

The name says
it all. Magical
blues from the
'20s on old 78s
that crackle like
curious flames.

Spicy Chicken Skewers

4 servings

Chicken skewers are a smart choice when you're in a hurry. Mix the marinade before you go to the beach and the job's half done. The actual grilling takes no time at all.

Directions

1. Cut the chicken into cubes and place in a bowl.

2. Mix all the ingredients for the marinade in another bowl. Pour the mix over the chicken and rub in thoroughly. Place the chicken in double plastic bags and refrigerate for at least 2 hours.

3. Make the dipping sauce: Mix together BBQ sauce, yogurt, and lime zest. Add salt and Tabasco to taste.

4. Thread the chicken onto skewers. Remember to soak the skewers for 30 minutes before use.

5. Grill rapidly over direct heat until the chicken begins to brown. Move over to indirect heat and continue to grill with lid on until cooked, a maximum of 5 minutes.

4 chicken fillets

Marinade

$\frac{1}{2}$ to 1 tbsp chipotle paste or smoked paprika

1 lime, grated zest and juice

$\frac{1}{2}$ c (1 dl) tomato juice

2 inches (5 cm) fresh ginger, grated

1 tsp cinnamon

1-2 tsp liquid smoke or brewed lapsang souchong tea

$\frac{1}{2}$ tsp allspice

2 tsp honey

2 tbsp soy sauce

$\frac{1}{4}$ c ($\frac{1}{2}$ dl) olive oil

Dipping sauce

$\frac{1}{2}$ c (1 dl) BBQ sauce of your choice, preferably "smoky" or "hickory"

1 c (2 dl) Turkish yogurt (or any plain yogurt)

1 lime, zest

salt

Tabasco, preferably chipotle flavor

Salmon Burger Deluxe

4 servings

A ridiculously tasty, not to mention effortless, alternative for those who find grilling fish a bit of a chore.

Directions

1. Cut the salmon into cubes.

2. Pulse the salmon, green onions, garlic, peeled ginger, chipotle, soy sauce, and sesame oil in a blender. Alternatively, chop very finely by hand.

3. Add bread crumbs and sesame seeds and mix carefully by hand.

4. Form the mixture into 4 patties. Make a small indentation in the middle of each. Season on both sides with salt and pepper. Allow to rest in the refrigerator for at least 1 hour. Brush with oil.

5. Meanwhile make the dressing: Mix the mayonnaise, sweet chili, yogurt, horseradish, and grated lime zest. Season with salt to taste.

6. Make sure that the grill is thoroughly cleaned and oil it well. You can even use a well-oiled grill basket. Grill the burgers over direct heat for 5 minutes. Pick up and flip carefully with a grill spatula. Grill the buns during the final minute.

7. Cover the bottoms of the buns with lettuce, and top with the burger, dressing, tomato, and cilantro. Put the top on and enjoy right away.

1 lb 2 oz (500 g) salmon fillets, boneless and skinless

4 green onions, sliced

3 garlic cloves

$1\frac{1}{2}$-2 inches (3-5 cm) fresh ginger

1 tsp chipotle paste

2 tbsp soy sauce

1 tbsp sesame oil

2/5 c (1 dl) day-old white bread crumbs

2 tbsp sesame seeds

salt

freshly ground black pepper

oil

Dressing

2 tbsp mayonnaise

2 tbsp sweet chili sauce

$\frac{1}{2}$ c (1 dl) Turkish yogurt (or any plain yogurt)

2 tsp horseradish, grated

zest of 1 lime

salt

Fixings

hamburger buns

lettuce

tomato, sliced

fresh cilantro

Margarita Shrimp

4 servings

I love shrimp and, well, a Margarita is my favorite drink. So I got my two loves together for a date on the grill. They were crazy about each other.

Directions

1. Mix all the marinade ingredients together in a bowl. Add the shrimp and rub in thoroughly. Cover with plastic wrap and allow to stand in the refrigerator for 2–3 hours.

2. Lift out the shrimp and throw the marinade away. Thread onto skewers, presoaked if you're using wooden ones.

3. Melt butter in a saucepan. Add Tabasco, garlic, and lime juice. Add salt to taste and keep warm.

4. Grill the shrimp over direct heat for about 3 minutes, turning occasionally. Plate up the skewers.

5. Pour over the melted butter and serve at once, preferably with good bread and a fresh salad.

1 lb 12 oz (800 g) large shrimp, peeled

Marinade

$\frac{1}{2}$ c (1 dl) tequila

$\frac{2}{5}$ c (1 dl) cilantro, coarsely chopped

$\frac{1}{2}$ c (1 dl) olive oil

2 garlic cloves, grated

1 jalapeno, chopped

2 tbsp Cointreau or Triple Sec

1 tbsp lime juice

Tabasco butter

3.5 oz (100 g) butter

1 tsp Tabasco

2 garlic cloves, chopped

1 lime, juiced

salt

Fabulous Veggie Burgers

4 servings

Yes you can get frozen veggie burgers at the store. Yes, they are quick and convenient. But tasty? Nah...try these instead, you won't regret it. Replace the dressing with the strawberry salsa (page 119) if you're a vegan.

Directions

1. Sauté the onions with a little salt and oil in a saucepan until they soften and become translucent and slightly golden. Add the garlic at the end.

2. Pour in the bulgur and water and cook, covered, on low heat until all the water has been absorbed, about 15 minutes. Pour into a bowl and add the beans and soy sauce.

3. Pulse the bulgur mixture in a blender with walnuts, fresh herbs, cumin, chipotle, pepper, and eggs (or cornstarch) until you get a smooth paste.

4. Form into 4 patties and allow to rest in the refrigerator for at least 30 minutes.

5. Make the dressing: Mix together mayonnaise, yogurt, grated lime zest, and lime juice. Add a little salt and Tabasco to taste.

6. Brush the burgers and the grill (or grill basket) with a little oil. Grill over direct heat for a couple of minutes on each side, turning carefully.

7. Grill the bread slices. Top with a burger, dressing, onion, tomato, and arugula. Top with another slice of bread if you like. Serve at once.

---

1 yellow onion, finely chopped

salt

olive oil

3 garlic cloves, finely chopped

$\frac{2}{5}$ c (1 dl) bulgur

1 c (2 dl) water

1 can (14 oz / 400 g) borlotti beans, rinsed and drained

1 tbsp soy sauce

$\frac{1}{5}$ c ($\frac{1}{2}$ dl) walnuts

1 bunch fresh cilantro or basil

$\frac{1}{5}$ c ($\frac{1}{2}$ dl) fresh mint, chopped or 1 tbsp dried

2 tsp cumin

1 to 2 tsp chipotle paste

freshly ground black pepper

2 eggs (or $\frac{2}{5}$ c [1 dl] cornstarch if you're vegan)

Dressing

$\frac{1}{4}$ c ($\frac{1}{2}$ dl) mayonnaise

$\frac{1}{4}$ c ($\frac{1}{2}$ dl) Turkish yogurt (or any plain yogurt)

1 lime, zest and juice

salt

Tabasco, preferably chipotle flavor

Fixings

coarse sourdough bread

red onion

tomato

arugula

A LITTLE TIP!

Leftover sauce can be stored in a glass jar in the refrigerator for up to 2 weeks.

Tender Ribs Country Style

4 servings

Grilling in reverse. Give your ribs color and flavor on the grill before braising them in the oven in a rich tomato sauce until they become wonderfully flaky and tender.

Directions

1. Heat the oven to 350 degrees F (175 degrees C).

2. Fry the bacon in a skillet on medium heat until the fat begins to melt. Add the garlic and onions and continue to fry while stirring until the onions soften.

3. Add chipotle, tomatoes, sugar, vinegar, mustard, Worcestershire sauce, cumin, salt, and pepper. Bring to a boil and allow to simmer for 5 minutes.

Set aside.

4. Season the ribs with salt and pepper. Grill over direct heat on an oiled grill until they achieve a nice color all over, around 8–10 minutes.

5. Transfer the meat to a roasting pan or ovenproof dish. Pour the tomato sauce over. Cook in the oven until the meat feels flaky and tender when you test it with a sharp knife, around 1 hour. Garnish with thyme if desired, and serve with Mia's Finest BBQ Sauce and a tasty salad, for example Black Bean Salad (page 95).

5 oz (140 g) bacon

4 garlic cloves, finely chopped

½ yellow onion, finely chopped

1-2 tsp chipotle paste or chipotle in adobo

1 can (14 oz / 400 g) crushed tomatoes

1 can (14 oz / 400 g) diced tomatoes

½ c (1 dl) brown sugar

½ c (1 dl) apple cider vinegar

4 tbsp coarse-grained mustard

1 tbsp Worcestershire sauce

1 tbsp cumin

2 tsp salt

freshly ground black pepper

about 2 lb 10 oz (1.2 kg) short ribs

fresh thyme to garnish if needed

Mia's Finest BBQ Sauce

1 substantial batch

I'm as proud of this sauce as I am of my children. Well, almost.

Directions

1. Sauté the onion gently with the oil in a saucepan without allowing them to color.

2. Add the chili sauce, HP sauce, vinegar, tomato juice, jelly, molasses, Worcestershire sauce, liquid smoke, cinnamon, cocoa, and allspice. Allow to simmer for a while then season with paprika or ancho, cayenne, and a little salt.

3. Simmer for 15 minutes. Allow to cool somewhat, then blend.

4. Serve cold or lukewarm with grilled meats.

1 small red onion, finely chopped

2 tbsp canola oil

½ c (1 dl) chili sauce, ketchup style

¼ c (½ dl) HP sauce

½ c (½ dl) apple cider vinegar

¾ c (1½ dl) tomato juice

¼ c (½ dl) black currant jelly

2 tbsp light molasses

2 tbsp Worcestershire sauce

1 tsp liquid smoke

2 tsp cinnamon

2 tsp cocoa

1 tsp allspice

1 tsp smoked paprika, or ancho chili powder

½-1 tsp cayenne pepper

salt

Sweet and Sticky Ribs

4 servings

Irresistibly tender, sticky ribs with tons of flavor. Arm yourself with extra napkins and eat till you drop.

Directions

1. Place the ribs in a large pot, splitting them if required. Cover with water. Add onion, vinegar, liquid smoke, salt, and bay leaves. Simmer, covered, until the meat feels tender when tested with a sharp knife, around 45–60 minutes. Remove from the heat and allow to cool.

2. Mix all the ingredients for the glaze. Brush the ribs with generous quantities of the mixture.

3. Grill over direct heat (move to indirect heat if they begin to look burned) until you get a nice outer crust, around 3–5 minutes. Brush with extra glaze during grilling. Serve with a fresh salad.

about 2 lb 3 oz (1 kg) baby back ribs

1 yellow onion, cut in wedges

2 tbsp apple cider vinegar

2-3 tbsp liquid smoke

$\frac{1}{2}$ tsp salt

2 bay leaves

Glaze

1 tsp coriander

2 star anise pods

1 tsp allspice

5 whole cloves

1 tsp cinnamon

$\frac{1}{2}$ tsp salt

$\frac{1}{2}$ tsp black pepper

1 tsp smoked paprika

$\frac{1}{2}$ c (1 dl) hoisin sauce (find it in the Asian food section)

$\frac{1}{2}$ c (1 dl) soy sauce

4 tbsp apple cider vinegar

4 tbsp honey

3 garlic cloves, grated

Triple Smoky Burger
4 servings

A smoky burger with extra everything. This could very well be the best burger in the world. According to me, anyway.

Directions

1. Mix the ground beef with the chipotle, paprika, liquid smoke, and a little salt. Form into 4 patties.
2. Make the dressing: Mix the mayonnaise, yogurt, mustard, BBQ sauce, chipotle, and grated lime zest. Add salt and a little lime juice to taste.
3. Slice the red onion into rings. Push in a toothpick to hold them together. Brush the onion rings and avocado with oil.
4. Fry or grill the bacon until it's crisp. Drain on paper towels.
5. Grill the onion rings on direct heat for 1–2 minutes on each side. Remove the toothpicks.
6. Grill the avocado wedges rapidly on each side.
7. Grill the burgers over direct heat for around 3–5 minutes on each side.
8. Split the hamburger buns and warm them quickly on the grill. Place the lettuce and burger on each bun and top with dressing, bacon, avocado, red onion, and basil. Enjoy!

1 lb 5 oz (600 g) ground beef

1 tbsp canned chipotle, chopped, or 2-3 tsp chipotle paste

2 tsp smoked paprika

$\frac{1}{2}$ tsp liquid smoke

salt

1 large red onion

1 avocado, cut into wedges

olive oil

8 strips smoked side bacon

Dressing

$\frac{1}{2}$ c (1 dl) mayonnaise

$\frac{1}{2}$ c (1 dl) Turkish yogurt (or any plain yogurt)

$1\frac{1}{2}$ tbsp Dijon mustard

2 tbsp smoky BBQ sauce, e.g., "hickory"

1 tbsp canned chipotles, chopped, or 2-3 tsp chipotle paste

1 lime

salt

Strawberry Salsa

4 servings

A summer salsa, halfway between a salad and a sauce. This is just made for the barbeque, whether you're grilling meat or fish.

Directions

1. Carefully blend the strawberries, avocadoes, mango, tomatoes, jalapenos, and green onions.

2. Squeeze the lime juice over the mixture. Add cilantro, cumin, and olive oil. Mix gently using your hands. Season with salt and, if required, extra lime to taste. Blend again.

3. Allow to stand and deepen in flavor in the refrigerator for an hour while you prepare the grill.

2 c ($\frac{1}{2}$ l) strawberries, halved

2 avocadoes, diced

1 ripe mango, diced (or frozen, defrosted)

2-3 perfect ripe tomatoes, diced

1-2 jalapenos, deseeded and finely chopped

1 bunch green onions, sliced

2-3 limes

1 bunch fresh cilantro, coarsely chopped

$\frac{1}{2}$ tsp cumin

2 tbsp olive oil

salt

Catharina

SETUP FOR A GRILL PARTY

The great thing about a grill party is that you can invite a whole lot of people and they probably won't have very high expectations when it comes to the table settings and decorations. That makes it even more fun to try and surprise them by making an extra effort.

During the warm summer grilling season when everything is growing, nature provides plenty of ideas for table decoration.

And fruit, vegetables, and flowers are at their best. Create something unexpected and decorate the table with charcoal! Give people something to talk about over dinner.

You can even make small table-setting kits if a group of you are planning a picnic to that romantic spot. If you're celebrating a special holiday why not tie the cutlery and paper plates up in a beautiful silk bow? Festive yet simple.

Catharina Lindeberg-Bernhardsson

Decorate with Charcoal

Why not use the charcoal as a table decoration? Put it in a length of rain gutter (available in hardware stores) to act as a table runner. Then light up that dark grill night by placing loads of tealights in the charcoal.

Directions

1. Cover the table with the tarp.

2. Put the end caps on the gutter and fill with charcoal. Place it along the middle of the table with a few flat stones underneath for it to stand on. Place the tealights in the charcoal.

3. Set the table with plates, cutlery, and wine glasses.

4. Fold the napkins into pockets (see photo): Lay out the napkin flat, fold it so it's half as big, fold once more so the bottom edge is about 4 inches. Fold back both ends, place the napkin on the plate, and put a fresh chili pepper in the pocket.

5. Decorate the table with dried chili peppers.

You'll need

a black tarp to cover the entire table

a length of silver-colored rain gutter

2 gutter end caps

charcoal, preferably ecological

some flat stones

tealights

porcelain plates, preferably old

silver cutlery

wine glasses

white linen napkins

fresh chili peppers in various colors

dried chili peppers in various colors

Recycled Table Settings

Make it easy when you're setting the table for your grill party by recycling newspapers and empty wine bottles. What could be more practical and beautiful? And the tablecloth can be as big as you like . . .

Directions

1. Remove the labels from the bottles by soaking in hot water and scrubbing. Pick plants with long stems; in the photo I've used thistles. When placing the bottles bear in mind that everybody should be able to see each other across the table.

2. Place candles in some of the bottles instead of flowers, or why not both...?

3. Tape the sheets of newspaper together to make a tablecloth.

empty wine bottles

long-stemmed flowers and plants

newspapers

tape

Edible Table Decorations

Decorate the table with fresh herbs to serve with the food. Place a small pair of scissors next to each place setting. The coarse burlap in the pictures was bought at a garden store. Finer material in the same color can be bought at fabric stores.

Directions

1. Lay the cloth on the table, overlapping sections if needed. Set places with plates, drinking glasses, and preferably beautiful crystal glasses to create a nice contrast with the coarse burlap.
2. Roll the cutlery in napkins, tie with string, and place perpendicular to the plate. Place scissors to the right of every place setting.
3. Wrap the pots a little carelessly in brown paper, tape, and roll down the edges. Place the pots along the center of the table in any old order, as a table runner.

A LITTLE TIP!

If you don't have napkins in burlap colors you can buy fabric and cut it to size. Hem it if you like but, hey, it's only a grill party . . .

A
LITTLE
TIP!

Always pack a
roll of paper
towels when you
picnic.

Place-Setting Kits

Paper plates and plastic glasses make life easier when you have lots of guests but use real cutlery as it works much better with grilled food than plastic. Parcel everything up in dish towels or paper napkins as a place-setting kit. Replace the string with ribbon for special occasions.

Directions

1. Wrap the cutlery in a dish towel and place on a paper plate along with a plastic glass.
2. Tie with brown string or ribbon, as seen in the photo, so that it's all held together.

You'll need

paper plates

plastic glasses

cutlery

dish towels or paper napkins

brown string/thin ribbon

Hydrangea Wreath

Take a hydrangea wreath along when you're going to grill somewhere else. It's easy to make and lasts for ages.

Directions

1. Soak the foam ring, allowing the ring to sit and soak. Don't press it down in the water.

2. Clip the hydrangea stalks to 1½ to 2 inches in length, and stick them into the ring until it's covered. Divide the plants if they're too large.

3. If you like you can stick a few other plants in among the hydrangeas. Here I've used some thistles and blooming lilac.

4. Stick hydrangea leaves into the outside of the ring.

You'll need

1 round floral foam ring

10-15 hydrangea flowers, depending on the size of the flowers and wreath

other flowers/plants if desired

hydrangea leaves

Flower Bouquet

Pick a bouquet for the party and fill a beautiful bowl. If you come across an abandoned fruit tree along the way, take a few sprigs to add, preferably with the apples or pears still on.

Directions

1. Put the shrubs in first as a base. Spread the flowers out evenly among the foliage.

You'll need

clippings from leafy shrubs

mixed picked flowers

Rosehip Basket

The beautiful red rosehip goes perfectly with a fiery grill.

Use gardening gloves to handle the thorny rosehip branches. Make one large or several smaller arrangements, maybe using various sizes of vase. Very sophisticated.

Directions

1. Soak the piece of foam for a few seconds, without pressing it down, so it can soak up the water. Push it down into the vase, bowl, etc.
2. Clip the rosehip branches to about 6 inches and sharpen the ends. Stick the branches into the foam at an angle to fill out the vase, bowl, or basket.

basket, bowl, vase, etc.

1 piece floral foam to fill

7-8 rosehip branches

Tomato Garland

Decorate with a garland of tomatoes of different shapes and colors. Fill the hole in the middle with small cocktail tomatoes, and then all that's left to do is eat the table setting!

Directions

1. Fasten the tomatoes to the wreath with grill skewers. Make a mix of colors and small and large tomatoes.

You'll need

tomatoes, preferably in various colors and sizes

grill skewers

straw wreath form

A LITTLE TIP!

It's even easier if you put a roll of paper towels in a basket so everyone can help themselves...or put a pile of paper napkins under a rock on the table.

Wild West Table Setting

Corn picked straight from the field can be a lovely table decoration, especially with the husks still on. An armful of sunflowers can also add to that rural western feel. If you're lucky enough to come across a field of sunflowers don't forget to ask the land owner's permission before you pick them. Put these magnificent flowers in a bucket of water and place that inside a large basket.

Directions

1. Lay the burlap over the table and the patterned fabric over that.
2. Set the table with plates, glasses, and cutlery.
3. Tie some of the ears of corn together in groups of three with brown string and place out as table decorations.
4. Place the napkins in a basket: fold the dish rags, and roll up the white cloth napkins and tie with string.
5. Prune the corn stalks and sunflowers to about the same length, and place in water, preferably leaning slightly to give an even shape.

You'll need

burlap

patterned fabric

plates

glasses

cutlery

cobs of corn

brown string

baskets

eco-friendly dish rags, various colors

white cloth napkins

corn stalks

sunflowers

bucket

large basket, if required

Boxed Wine Bundle

When there are a lot of guests it's handy to have a box of wine. Practical, but maybe not so pretty. So why not bundle the box up in burlap? After that, if you can arrange some hay bales to set it on, then you've got yourself a real country bar.

Directions

1. Wrap the wine box in burlap and tie with string (see photo).

You'll need

burlap

brown string

hay bales

GRILLED DESSERTS

When grilling desserts we're not usually after that smoky taste or that lovely, slightly burned effect that one tries to achieve when grilling meat and vegetables. Here it's all about using heat to make fruit even more juicy and full of flavor, caramelizing marshmallows, and toasting cakes and other treats.

Personally I mostly use a propane grill, partly because I live in an apartment and don't want to disturb the neighbors with too much smoke, and also because I find it simple and practical. It's so much easier to motivate yourself when the grill warms up in moments without all that waiting around for the embers to start glowing. You can grill more and for longer without having to worry about the fire burning out just as you're about to prepare dessert. Some people maintain that you might just as well fry the food in a pan as use a propane grill and up to a point I can understand what they mean, but blind tests have shown that most people can't tell the difference between meat cooked on a propane grill or over charcoal.

The desserts in this chapter work equally well done on propane as on coals and a couple of them, such as s'mores and backpack bananas, can simply be grilled over a campfire. Don't be afraid to try your own experiments either. Pretty much everything tastes better after a turn on the grill.

In the unlikely event that you're tired of grilling by the time you've fixed the main course, I'm even going to share a few of my absolute favorite recipes for summer desserts made off the grill. Round off the meal with blueberry ice cream cones, homemade strawberry crème, rhubarb crumble, or another one of my favorites.

Mia Öhrn

Grilled Peaches
with Coconut & Chocolate

4 servings

Peaches are among the tastiest treats of the whole summer. You can vary this dish by using nectarines and white or dark chocolate.

Directions

1. Mix the coconut flakes with the chocolate and soft butter.

2. Halve the peaches and remove the pits.

3. Lay the peaches cut side down on a fairly hot grill. After a couple of minutes turn them over and divide the coconut mixture among them, placing it in the middle of each half. Continue to grill for around 10–15 minutes or until the fruit softens. Serve with vanilla ice cream.

$\frac{2}{5}$ c (1 dl) coconut flakes

1 oz (25 g) milk chocolate, coarsely chopped

2 tbsp (25 g) butter, at room temperature

4 ripe peaches

vanilla ice cream to serve

S'mores

4 servings

The American classic. Childishly sweet and delicious!

Directions

1. Thread the marshmallows onto a skewer and grill until they get a little color. This works fine over coals or an open fire.

2. Put two pieces of chocolate and two grilled marshmallows on a graham cracker. Top with another cracker. Repeat. Serve immediately.

8 large marshmallows

8 pieces dark chocolate

8 graham cracker squares

Grilled Pineapple & Strawberry Skewers with Lime Dip

4 servings

This fruit skewer is great just as it is but when the strawberries and fresh pineapple are heated it really brings out the flavors.

Directions

1. Lime dip: Mix the lime zest and yogurt. Add confectioner's sugar a little at a time to sweeten dip to taste. Allow to stand in a cold place until served.

2. Fruit skewers: Slice off the top and bottom from the pineapple. Peel off the skin, and quarter. Remove the hard core and cut into pieces.

3. Rinse and clean the strawberries and cut into halves or quarters.

4. Thread the fruit onto skewers and grill on a hot or medium grill until the fruit softens. Serve with the lime dip.

Lime dip

1 lime, finely grated zest

1 c (2 dl) yogurt

1-2 tbsp confectioner's sugar

Fruit skewers

1 pineapple

2 c ($\frac{1}{2}$ l) strawberries

Grilled Sponge Cake
with Raspberries

4 servings

Make use of leftover sponge cake by grilling it and serving it with whipped cream and summer berries.

4-8 slices sponge cake
$\frac{1}{4}$ c ($\frac{1}{2}$ dl) whipping cream
1 c (200 g) raspberries

Directions

1. Cut the sponge cake into slices, planning on 1–2 slices per person.

2. Whip the cream lightly, for a soft consistency.

3. Grill the sponge cake for a few minutes on each side over a hot or medium grill. Serve at once with the cream and raspberries.

Basic Sponge Cake Recipe

Directions

1. Heat oven to 350 degrees F (175 degrees C).

2. Butter an 8 x 8" cake pan. Coat bottom and sides with the bread crumbs.

3. Melt the butter.

4. Mix flour and baking powder.

5. Whip the eggs, vanilla, and sugar with an electric whisk until fluffy. Add in the flour mix a little at a time, alternating with the butter and milk. Mix carefully together into a smooth batter using a hand whisk.

6. Pour the cake batter into the pan and bake on the lowest rack of the oven for about 40 minutes. Turn the cake pan upside down onto parchment paper or a cooling rack, and allow to cool for a few minutes before removing the pan.

butter and fine bread crumbs for the pan
5 tbsp (75 g) butter
$1\frac{1}{2}$ c (180 g) flour
1 tsp baking powder
3 eggs
$\frac{1}{2}$ tsp vanilla extract
1 c (2 dl) sugar
$\frac{3}{4}$ c ($1\frac{1}{2}$ dl) milk

Backpack Bananas

4 servings

A modern classic that tastes just as good at home on the grill as it does around the campfire.

4 bananas, in skins
3 oz (100 g) milk chocolate
vanilla ice cream to serve

Directions

1. Cut a slit along the length of the banana as shown in the photo.

2. Stick 3–4 pieces of chocolate into each slit and wrap each banana in foil.

3. Grill for about 10 minutes over medium heat or until the bananas begin to soften and smell good. You can even place the bananas directly in the smoldering embers.

Grilled Baked Alaska

4 servings

Wrapping the ice cream in filo pastry gives enough protection to allow it to be grilled without melting. If you use ice cream from a rectangular package it makes it easier to divide up. Outside of the grilling season these ice cream packages are also very good fried quickly in butter and a little sugar in a hot skillet.

$3\frac{1}{2}$ tbsp (50 g) butter
1 qt (1 l) vanilla ice cream
4 sheets filo pastry
fresh berries to serve

Directions

1. Melt the butter. Cut the ice cream into four pieces.

2. Brush the first filo pastry sheet with thin layer of butter. Wrap up a piece of ice cream in the sheet, and brush the outside with melted butter. Repeat with the rest of the ice cream and sheets of pastry. Place the 4 pastry packages in the freezer for at least 15 minutes to make sure that the ice cream freezes completely again.

3. Grill quickly on a hot grill on all sides. Serve immediately, preferably with fresh summer berries.

Strawberry Crème with Milk

4-5 servings

Homemade crème is really something special! Serve with milk and homemade macaroons.

Directions

1. Rinse and clean the strawberries and cut them fairly small.

2. Mix the strawberries with the cordial, water, and sugar in a saucepan.

3. Bring to a boil and allow to boil for 3–4 minutes, whisking occasionally.

4. Mix the potato flour with water and mix it into the boiling crème. Whisk vigorously until it begins to thicken and bubble again. Remove from the heat and allow to cool slightly.

2 c (about $\frac{1}{2}$ l) strawberries

$\frac{1}{2}$ c (1 dl) diluted red cordial, e.g., strawberry, mixed, or rhubarb

2 c (4 dl) water

2 tbsp sugar

$1\frac{1}{2}$ tbsp potato flour + 2 tbsp water

Macaroons

30-40 small cookies

Directions

1. Heat the oven to 350 degrees F (175 degrees C).

2. Work the egg white into the almond paste with your hands or a food processor.

3. Line an oven tray with parchment paper and pipe out tiny cookies. You can also dollop out the mixture using two small spoons. Dip the spoons in water often to prevent sticking. The cookies don't need to be flat or good looking — they'll come together in the oven.

4. Bake in the middle of the oven for 8–10 minutes. Allow to cool, and serve with the strawberry crème.

2 tsp egg white

3.5 oz (100 g) almond paste

Rhubarb Crumble

6-8 servings

An 84-year-old lady, a very experienced baking enthusiast indeed, taught me to cut through the acid flavor of the rhubarb by adding some apple. Of course, if you prefer, you can make it with just rhubarb.

Directions

1. Heat the oven to 350 degrees F (175 degrees C).

2. Crumble: Measure out the flour, oats, and salt in a bowl and add the cold butter in small pieces. Finely blend the butter into the flour with your fingertips and press it together into a crumbly mixture. Work in the sugar. It also works perfectly well if you mix it all together in a food processor.

3. Filling: Cut the rhubarb into half-inch pieces. Peel and core the apple and cut into small pieces. Mix the fruit together with the potato flour.

4. Scatter half of the crumble mixture over the bottom of a pie dish. Spread the fruit over it and top with the rest of the crumble.

5. Bake on the bottom rack of the oven for about 50 minutes or until golden brown. Allow to cool, and serve, preferably with vanilla ice cream.

Crumble

1 c (120 g) flour

1 c (2 dl) rolled oats

$\frac{1}{5}$ tsp salt

$\frac{3}{4}$ c (175 g) butter, straight from the fridge

$\frac{1}{2}$ c (1 dl) sugar

Filling

14 oz (400 g) rhubarb

1 medium sized apple

2 tsp potato flour

Blueberry Parfait Cones

10-12 cones

A homemade ice cream cone to round off the barbeque will put a smile on the faces of young and old alike. For a little variation make the parfait with raspberries or strawberries instead.

Directions

1. Place the cones in glasses or something similar so they are stable. Make sure that they'll fit upright in the freezer.

2. Mix the blueberries finely in a blender or with a hand mixer. Stir in the vanilla.

3. Whip the cream in a bowl until it's fluffy and firm but not too stiff.

4. In another bowl whisk the egg yolks and sugar with an electric whisk until really pale and fluffy.

5. Fold the blueberry mixture into the whipped cream with a spatula. Carefully do the same with the egg mixture and mix to a paste.

6. Pour, pipe, or spoon the mixture into the cones. Freeze for at least 2 hours.

7. Allow the parfait in the cones to soften slightly before serving. Garnish with whipped cream, sprinkles, and a wafer.

10-12 wafer cones

10 oz (275 g) blueberries, fresh, or frozen and defrosted

1 tsp vanilla extract

$1\frac{1}{2}$ c (3 dl) whipping cream

4 egg yolks

$\frac{1}{4}$ c ($\frac{1}{2}$ dl) sugar

whipped cream, sprinkles, and wafers to serve

Elderberry Marinated Strawberries with Cream & Chocolate Crisp

Makes about 4 servings

Possibly the summer's easiest and most delicious dessert!

Directions

1. Chocolate crisp: Carefully melt the chocolate in the microwave or over a water bath. Mix in the cereal flakes and spread the mixture out on a board covered with greaseproof or parchment paper. Allow to set in the refrigerator.

2. Elderberry marinated strawberries: Rinse and clean the strawberries and cut into small pieces. Mix with the diluted cordial and allow to marinate for about 20 minutes. Lightly whip the cream.

3. Break up the chocolate crisp into small pieces and layer with the cream and strawberries in glasses or single-serving bowls. Garnish with wild strawberry leaves if desired. Serve immediately.

Chocolate crisp

3 oz (75 g) dark chocolate

1 c (2 dl) Special K, or similar cereal

Elderberry marinated strawberries

2 c ($\frac{1}{2}$ l) strawberries

2 tbsp elderberry cordial, diluted

$\frac{3}{4}$ c (1$\frac{1}{2}$ dl) whipped cream to serve

Oven Pan Pie with Blueberries & Raspberries

Makes about 12-14 slices

A pastry that's a cross between a pie and a soft cake, and on top of that is easy to bake and goes a long way.

Directions

1. Heat the oven to 350 degrees F (175 degrees C).

2. In a bowl measure out the flour, baking powder, salt, and sugar. Add the butter in small pieces and work into the flour mixture with your fingertips until you get a crumbly mixture.

3. Whisk the egg and milk together and mix into the flour mixture. Work it quickly into a fairly loose pastry. You can even mix it together in a food processor.

4. Roll the dough out about half an inch thick on a floured board and transfer it onto a baking sheet lined with parchment paper. If it feels particularly sticky roll it out directly onto the paper.

5. Mix the berries with sugar and potato flour and spread over the dough.

6. Bake the pie in the middle of the oven for about 30 minutes or until the edges get some color and the berries begin to bubble.

Pie dough

3$\frac{1}{2}$ c (420 g) flour

1 tbsp baking powder

$\frac{1}{2}$ tsp salt

$\frac{3}{4}$ c (1$\frac{1}{2}$ dl) sugar

1$\frac{1}{2}$ c (350 g) butter, straight from the fridge

2 eggs

$\frac{1}{2}$ c (1 dl) milk, sour cream, or yogurt

Filling

9 oz (250 g) blueberries

9 oz (250 g) raspberries

$\frac{1}{4}$ c ($\frac{1}{2}$ dl) sugar

1 tbsp potato flour

SURE-FIRE WINES

Bengt-Göran Kronstam

It was on the second of July, 1964, that I discovered the phenomenal flavors of barbequed meats, and I've been a devoted disciple of the art ever since. That same morning I had, together with my parents and brother, landed in New York for the first time. I was twelve years old and I remember it as if it were yesterday. The taste sensation was so overwhelming, the aromas alone turning the whole thing into a ritual that I continue to sanctify as often as the opportunity presents itself and not just during the summer months. I've been known to light the grill with the snow lying deep around the porch.

At home in Sweden back then, it was still traditional fare on the dinner table every day. On special occasions we ate ham with mimosa salad, pork noisettes, at best sole Walewska or fillet of veal in Béarnaise sauce. On both sides of the Atlantic there was still a long way to go before the realization that wine is a supreme mealtime drink. I myself was partial to lemonade and raspberry soda, but that was due to my age of course. The Americans drank cocktails and coffee, even with meals. The Swedes? Beer and snaps (schnapps), wine only in exceptional circumstances and then more because it was considered fancy than because it tasted good. Today that's all in the past.

In recent years our cuisine in Sweden has come closer to a depth of flavor more reminiscent of the intensity of the barbeque, in contrast to the traditional slow cooking's milder and more nuanced taste palette. Wines on the whole have also developed in the same direction, with more body and a higher alcohol content. This development has also bought with it a more distinct experience of both roundness and sweetness, something that is ideally suited to grilled food.

Therefore choosing a wine doesn't need to be daunting. In fact, right and wrong is something you can more or less forget about. When it comes to wine there's a much greater chance that, whatever you pop the cork on, it will taste good rather than not. Whatever the old rules of etiquette or the opinions of hard-to-please wine snobs, choose the wines you enjoy. These, as a rule, will taste the best.

Having said that, there are a number of shortcuts to reaching the ultimate taste experience. Above all this applies to the acidity of the wine. It's the acidity that gives wine its freshness and breaks through the salt and fat, especially important if you choose a really full bodied, highly extracted wine. Without acidity the wine will satiate the appetite rather than whet it.

BARBEQUE IS GOOD! Whether you use a spicy BBQ sauce or a parrilla á la Argentinian asado, the wine is a spice that's hard to do without. Sure a beer tastes good while you're waiting for the food to cook but, with the food itself, wine is much more festive.

On the whole, grilling gives food more character and flavor. Therefore the wines that go with it should follow the same formula. Otherwise, the more elegant tastes risk being lost. A mild sweetness or grapiness and a relatively high intense alcohol content usually give the best results.

Grilling is also a part of picnicking, boating, and camping. On these occasions a box wine might seem like the wisest choice. In that case, make sure that you buy a fresh box! To be on the safe side, six months after the filling date is the recommended shelf life for a red wine, and for white wine and rosé four months, even if the suppliers are inclined to be more optimistic. Don't buy more than you need at one time. Store the box in the refrigerator until it's finished. The temperature of the wine will rise quickly in the glass anyway and a cool wine is much more refreshing than a tepid one.

Even at home it's best to serve wine at a lower than ambient temperature, whether that be in a room, on the deck, on the balcony, or wherever you may find yourself. Rosé and white wines should be chilled in an ice bucket or the refrigerator.

AMONG THE TASTE TYPES there are two that dominate. On the white side there are the rounded and generous, and among red wines we have the spicy and full bodied.

The similarities between these two types are striking, even if the colors are different. Here you have warm and well-rounded wines, often with a clear tone of dark, toasted oak. These often come from the so-called new world and it's in these countries that barbequing is most widespread.

However, you don't have to have crunchy explosions of fruit just because you're grilling. Even among other taste types there are wines that are both drinkable and barbeque-friendly. This is especially true if you choose ingredients that emphasize the qualities of the wine, rather than choosing an off-the-shelf barbeque sauce. Onions, cheese, mushrooms, and tomatoes are among these. A creamy puree of, for example, celeriac, cauliflower, or Jerusalem artichokes can also do the trick.

You can even fix dessert over the grill's fiery coals. In that case the advice is the same; choose a fairly expressive wine, preferably with more freshness than sweetness. A sparkling rosé, such as Italian Rotari Rosé, or a luxurious champagne like Gosset Grand Rosé Brut, would be absolutely perfect, or if you want something really sweet, the sparkling Muscat wine Nivole from northern Italy.

CAN'T I DRINK BEER THEN? Of course you can and, in that case, the very same liberating advice applies. Let your own tastes and opinions decide. You can even drink soda, water (which should always be available, even when drinking wine, to quench thirst), juice, or hard cider if that's what you prefer.

For those who can't or don't want to drink alcohol there is now, in the form of Natureo Free Syrah, an alcohol free red that tastes of more than flat grape soda. If you prefer white try Natureo Free Muscat or the bubbly Schloss Boosenburg. For those of you who prefer rosé, you have a perfect alternative in Lancers Free Rosé.

Twelve Sure-Fire Winners for Your Grill Party

These wines maintain a high quality at reasonable prices. Some may need to be ordered in advance, but in return they'll be well worth the wait.

You may also view this list as a guide if you're interested in exploring new taste experiences. You'll find a lot of help is available along the way from your wine merchant. Choose a wine you enjoy from the list and ask them to recommend something in a similar style.

Box

WHITE: Garofoli Verdicchio dei Castelli di Jesi Classico
An excellent box available to order; also available in bottles at a great price.

RED: Allegrini Valpolicella Superiore
A modern reworked valpolicella, more generous with the fruit in this grill-friendly version.

ROSÉ: Vernissage Syrah Rosé
The best rosé box in this vintage.

Budget

WHITE: Viña Maipo Chardonnay
Chilean generosity produces sunshine in a bottle.

RED: Terre de Mistral
A well-made and very welcome acquaintance from the Rhone Valley.

ROSÉ: Puycheric Syraha
When tempted to try a rosé, it's the Riviera we always turn to.

Medium

WHITE: Casal di Serra
This faithful old Italian retainer works just as well with grilled fish, shellfish, and meat as it does with a salad.

RED: Langhe Nebbiolo Fontanafredda
Full of character, this powerhouse is perfect with that beautiful, charcoal grilled cut of meat.

ROSÉ: Domaine de Collavery
Making a paella on the grill? This is just the wine!

Luxury

WHITE: Neudorf Chardonnay Nelson
Complex and full of flavor, this delicious New Zealand wine is produced in a broad international style.

RED: Le Volte
This Italian wine has a beautifully tailored elegance, while retaining a bite that will make your grilled meats turn somersaults.

ROSÉ: Minuty Rosé
You'll be seduced by the curvaceous bottle, and the contents will not disappoint!

INDEX

INTRODUCING THE GRILL MASTERS

ULRIKA EKBLOM is a photographer. Her work includes books, magazines, and advertisements, primarily dealing with food and interior design. She shares a studio, as well as the online magazine *Le Parfait*, with Liselotte Forslin.

Her favorite grill nights are spent with friends and family on the beach in Gotland.

LISELOTTE FORSLIN is a food writer, recipe developer, food stylist, and cookbook author. She writes for magazines and newspapers and shares a studio and the online magazine *Le Parfait* with Ulrika Ekblom.

For her, the best thing about grilling is hanging out with good friends and relaxing with an ice cold beer in her hand while waiting for the grill to heat up.

MIA GAHNE is a food writer, freelance journalist, and translator. She styles, writes cookbooks, reports, and creates recipes for several newspapers and magazines. She was awarded The Gastronomic Academy's gold pen in 2011.

For her, happiness is a perfectly grilled burger with extra everything. She also firmly asserts that there's no such thing as "can't grill."

JAN GRADVALL is a prize winning music journalist. He writes for *Dagens Industri* and *Expressen Culture* among others and has published several books.

The thing he likes most about grilling is standing around the fire while choosing which music to play in the background.

INGELA HOLM is a publisher. She has been involved in many hundreds of cookbooks. In 2007 she traveled to China to accept a prize for her contribution as a member of the jury for the *Gourmand* World Cookbook Awards.

She grills all year round!

BENGT-GÖRAN KRONSTAM is the wine critic for *Dagens Nyheter* and associate editor at the magazine *Allt om Vin*. His book *the Magic of Wine* was voted the world's best wine book of 2007, and in 2008, *The Magic of Taste* was voted best combined food and wine book written in Sweden.

He has a declared preference for large cuts of meat grilled slowly, seasoned only with salt and pepper.

JONAS LARSSON is a graphic designer and art director. He works on books, graphic profiling, and lifestyle magazines. He has, among other things, produced a number of books together with his sister Liselotte Forslin and is the missing link in *Le Parfait*.

He has a complicated relationship with charcoal briquettes.

CATHARINA LINDEBERG-BERNHARDSSON is a table setting artist, course instructor, and lecturer. She has also written several books, among them *Seasonal Table Settings: 21 Designs Inspired by Nature* (Schiffer) and *Garlands All Year Round* (ICA Publishing).

She says that the best thing about a grill party is that you can invite a lot of people and that anything goes when it comes to setting the table.

TOVE NILSSON is a chef, sommelier, and food writer. She contributes to newspapers, cookbooks, and radio as well as holding courses in cooking and wine tasting.

She grills all summer. Everything from hot dogs to slow cooked dishes like pulled pork or BBQ ribs.

MIA ÖHRN is a pastry chef, food writer, and course instructor who, among other things, has published the book *Brownies* (ICA Publishing). She creates recipes for magazines, and runs the kitchen studio Matlabbet and the publishing house Parasoll.

Her earliest grill memory is being out with her family collecting cones to burn on that summer's grill fires.